THE
MUSIC
OF THE
BAROQUE

Cover design: From a wrought-iron
balcony pattern for the Palace at
Versailles, César Daly, architect, 1683.
Cover type: Goudy and Goudy Open.

THE MUSIC OF THE BAROQUE

Edith Borroff

Eastern Michigan University

WM. C. BROWN COMPANY PUBLISHERS
Dubuque, Iowa

Printed in the United States of America.

For my mother,
who taught me first
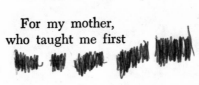

Contents

Preface

No historical period of music seems closer to modern times than the Baroque era. The inventiveness, the rhythmic propulsion, and the free-wheeling melodic variations of Baroque music are akin to jazz, swing, and rock, a kinship fully savored by today's musical public.

A summary of the music of the Baroque can not only suggest the splendor of that period, but it can assess the chief accomplishments of the era and point to the areas especially fruitful for listeners to explore further.

Examples of music are included—intended not alone for those who are familiar with musical notation—although the examples are self-contained and can be considered parenthetical. The main point of music is not the way it looks but the way it sounds, and for this an eager ear and open mind are the primary requisites. The look of a page of music has its own magic, and it reveals shapes and textures (and has overtones of intention and personality) whether or not its peruser is trained to read it. Thus examination of the examples is urged upon all hands.

I would like to thank Wallace S. Bjorke, Head Librarian of the School of Music Library of the University of Michigan, who has cheerfully extended exceptional courtesies in the use of Library materials, and the University of Michigan Photographic Services for their work in preparing the facsimiles.

I am particularly grateful to Michele and Jon Rinka, who helped with the typescript and gave generously of time and energy along the way.

Edith Borroff

List of Plates

List of Examples

At the Edge
of a
New Style

THE RENAISSANCE HERITAGE

he period of the history of Western Music which musicians call Baroque was a long one, stretching from the close of the sixteenth century well into the eighteenth century. Its music was rich, varied, and of a particular excitement because the Baroque era was an experimental one. Its musical inventions would be basic to the whole musical language of the Classical and Romantic periods, and must be re-appreciated as intensely creative innovations. In addition, the spirit of the seventeenth century had much in common with our own time: a new style of music was proposed, and over the span of several generations went from the radical to the fully accepted, while old styles and forms continued and were eventually modified by the new. Further, the Baroque century was an explorative one, particularly in the geographical, scientific, and political spheres. Seventeenth-century men, like men of today, felt the power of discovery, and were aware of being on the brink of new concepts of the world and of man.

Most Renaissance music had been polyphonic: conceived as having a specific number of written lines or "voices," proceeding either in a rhythmically unified fashion (called the *familiar style*) or in a rhythmically independent fashion (called the *learned style*). Musical structures had been based on the single phrase, associated with a line or phrase of text on the one hand or a unit of dance steps on the other; such a phrase unit was called a *punctus* (plural, *puncti*), or, in English, a *point*. Popular music centered in the familiar style in which words and dance rhythms were most clearly delineated; the *imitative point* was used occasionally in the popular style, but was more often reserved for longer, more complex forms, and for that reason was thought of as part of the *learned style*, as *worked* or elaborated music.

POLYPHONIC FORMS

The great polyphonic forms had been the *Mass ordinary*, the motet, and the *polyphonic chanson*. The Mass ordinary, a setting of the *Kyrie*, *Sanctus-Benedictus*, and *Agnus Dei* that were always included in the Mass, plus the *Credo* and *Gloria* (on joyful feasts), was the expansive, multimovement form of the Renaissance, most often based upon a preexistent melody, sacred or popular, placed in the tenor, and called the *cantus firmus* or fixed melody (the plural is *cantūs firmi*). The motet was a polyphonic setting of a sacred text; in the Anglican Church it was called an *anthem*, a shortened form of *antiphon*. Other Protestant churches, notably the German Lutherans and French *Huguenots*, concentrated on *hymns* and *Psalms* for singing at home as well as in church. These were generally simple and direct, often taken directly from popular songs and centering in the familiar style.

The *polyphonic chanson*, the chief popular form of the Renaissance, had begun as a courtly form, but as the Burgundian and Franco-Flemish composers of the fifteenth and early sixteenth centuries had fanned out through the cultural centers of central and southern Europe, the idea of multivoiced song had been translated into the vernaculars, so that the more-or-less universal French lyric gave way to local poetry and the music to local idiom. By the end of the Renaissance the *chanson* was a French song, while the German *Lied*, the Spanish *villancico*, the Italian *madrigal*, and the English *ayre* and *madrigal* (an importation of the Italian term) were well established as national types.

THE CONSORT

Renaissance performance had sought blended tones in unified quality: the *consort* was the ideal at the height of the Renaissance, a group of four, five, or six (as many as the lines of polyphony) instruments of the same kind but of different sizes; a group of recorders, viols, Krummhorns, for example, matched instruments of like quality in different sizes in emulation of vocal ranges. The *choir* and *vocal consort* sought the same blend; the church choir used three or four voices on each line, but music in the court or home continued, like the instrumental consort, to use one voice per line. The consort was a group of matched soloists. A consort might play a vocal work—notably a chanson—by using the part books of the singers; they might also play polyphonic dances.

Alongside of the central Renaissance concern with blend within the polyphonic work, a new kind of music had been gaining in popularity and confidence. Music directly composed for particular instruments, particularly for the lute—the most popular Renaissance instrument—and for the organ, was idiomatic and even virtuoso by the end of the sixteenth century. The *toccata, fantasia, variation* (most often the breaking of a melody into shorter note values, a technique called *division*), and *ricercar* (a searching—experimenting—piece), were probably the most popular of these forms. In addition, polyphonic music for the instrumental consort, based upon the chanson and named for it, had developed into complex types. At first Italian printers issued editions of popular chansons for instrumental consorts, using the translation *canzona francese*; then new works, copying the chanson, used the title *canzona alla francese* (chanson in the French style). By the end of the century, these were being composed for opposing consorts, separated spatially in performance in an architectural deployment exploited by the composers in alternating and combining the instrumental forces. In addition, the substitution of a contrasting instrument for a prominent—generally top —part in the consort became fashionable. This was called a *broken consort*; Giovanni Gabrieli's famed *Sonata pian' e forte* (the Soft and Loud Sonata) pitted two broken consorts against one another both musically and spatially: one group was composed of a *cornett* and three trombones, the other of a viola and three trombones. The *mixed consort,* of diverse instruments, all either *high* (meaning loud) or *low* (meaning soft), also came into prominence. The *cornett* was a wooden instrument, bound in leather, with finger holes and an ivory mouthpiece; it was versatile and widely used.

Such performing techniques were looking forward; practiced by the modernists, they would prove basic to the new styles of the Baroque.

A POLAR TEXTURE

Even more modern was the interest, late in the sixteenth century, in the solo voice, particularly in a dramatic or unusually poetic (rather than formalized) text. To an extent, the singer who sang to his lute produced the sound of a broken consort, but the whole theoretical concept of such a performance entailed a basic revision of the practical theory of the composition of music, and it was there that the basis of Baroque theory was to be defined. Early in the century, the lute player had played the bottom lines of a chanson while singing the top line as a solo song. The work was still a polyphonic chanson; its concept of composition was identical, and only its style of performance was changed. In contradistinction, at the end of the century the *lute song,*

Plate I

The *Consort*. A painting by Lorenzo Costa (c. 1460-1535). The singers seem to be maintaining a *tactus* (beat) by tapping their fingers. The small fiddle was called a *kit*, and was used by dancing teachers; the straight instrument was a flute. The carving in the center of the lute, often an ornate arabesque design, was called a rose hole; it served as a resonator.

solo Madrigal, or *air au luth* was conceived as a solo whose important musical line was balanced by the accompanying lines, with special reference to the bottom. The polarity of bottom and top lines imputed dramatic vitality to the top and structural vitality to the bottom, in a motivating fusion of separate function.

The polar concept of musical fabric was a radical reversal of the old theory in which the tenor had been considered the structurally motivating line, with other lines added around it. Not only was the vital element moved from the center of the fabric to two extremes, but also the melodic line of the tenor was taken away, replaced by a harmonic element which required certain chords to sound but regarded them as separate vertical elements, not as the result of specified linear interactions

Performance of the lute song mirrored the concept of structure by reinforcing the bottom line with a viola da gamba, leaving the clear melodic lines to the voice and the gamba, and using the lute to complete the harmonic dimension.

AT THE END OF THE RENAISSANCE

At the end of the Renaissance, two types of musical fabric were well established: the fabric of the consort, made up of separate lines, generally four, five, or six, often combined in antiphonal practice; and the fabric of the lute song, made up of two lines, treble and bass, with a middle ground conceived as fulfilling the harmonic implications of the bass. The first, whether familiar or imitative, was called *polyphony*, and it was a late development of a language with a heritage of centuries. The second, as developed in Italy in the last decade of the sixteenth century, was called *monody*. Both would flourish in the musical era to come, but monody would usher in a new style and announce the Baroque in music.

Suggestions for Further Study

Records

John Dowland: Ayres for Four Voices. Westminster, W-9619.

Lute Music from the Royal Courts of Europe. Julian Bream. RCA Victor, LM-2924.

Lute songs of Morley, Dowland, and Campion. Archive, ARC-3004.

The Renaissance Band. New York Pro Musica. Decca DL 79424. Contains a demonstration of consorts, broken consorts, and combined consorts.

Social Music in Italy: Madrigals of Marenzio and Gesualdo. Archive, ARC 3073.

Books and Music

GREENBERG, NOAH, music editor. *An Elizabethan Song Book.* Garden City, N.Y.: Doubleday Anchor Books, 1955. Contains lute songs transcribed directly and unchanged.

PRAETORIUS, MICHAEL. *The Syntagma Musicum.* English translation by Harold Blumenfeld. New York: Barenreiter, c. 1962. This is the second volume, on instruments, from a most valuable source, dating from 1618; it contains facsimiles of the original illustrations. Two of these appear as Plates II and VII.

STEVENS, DENIS (Ed.) *The Penguin Book of English Madrigals.* Penguin Books 033 (1967). Although the collection is in four parts, whereas five or six would be more representative of late Renaissance polyphony, the introduction and clean editing make this a good anthology for studying part song. Bateson's "Phyllis, Farewell" (#3, p. 22) is an example of the familiar style; Byrd's "This Sweet and Merry Month" (#8, p. 42) of the learned; and Farnaby's "Construe My Meaning" (#13, p. 70) of the chromatic madrigal long beloved of the Italians.

In addition, the *General Book List* on page 134 should be included for readings appropriate to this chapter and all succeeding chapters.

The New
Style in Italy

MONODY

he Italians of the late sixteenth century were vitally
interested in both the theatre and the artistic practices of
classical Greece. The *Teatro Olimpico* had opened near
Venice in 1585 with a performance of the Sophocles
Œdipus Rex complete with complex stage machinery,
lavish costuming, and incidental music—instrumental and
choral—by Andrea Gabrieli (c. 1520-1586), the uncle of Giovanni and director of music at St. Mark's Cathedral. The tantalizing statements of Aris-
totle and other Greek writers concerning the honored place of music in
Greek drama had led composers to an attempt at dramatic declamation
in music, to carry a text forward directly and naturally as words
heightened emotionally by music rather than embellished parenthetically
or in songs between spoken sections.

The new style was as much a manner of performance as of composition, and it is not surprising that among its first advocates were singers
as well as composers. The new style was called *monody*, a name its
proponents derived from the Greek meaning "singing alone"; the "alone"
referred to one singer (rather than a consort of singers), and did not
mean that the singer would sing without instruments. On the contrary,
the new concept of treble-bass polarity was found ideal for monodic
declamation and was vital to its musical reality. It was in Italy that
this musical reality was reflected in a new notation that made evident
the principle of the new style and also, in complementary omission,
made implicit its essential modernity and antipolyphony.

BASSO CONTINUO

The two linear elements of monody had two different functions: the primary declamatory and melodic elements resided in the top line, while the harmonic and structural elements, along with a vital balance to the top part, resided in the bass, which was necessarily constant and was called a *basso continuo* (later, in English, the *thoroughbass* or *general bass*). The treble could be written out as a solo line, or at least the bare bones of a solo line which the singer would *improve*—i.e., flesh out in improvized division and ornamentation. The bass could also be written out as a melody, since it was a balancing line to the top, though its harmonic function kept it from the melodic freedom of the solo line.

The harmonic aspect of the bass, however, gave it a twofold function that was reflected in its being performed most frequently by two people, one to play its melody as a balancing line to the solo, and the other to provide the harmonies which the bass implied. The first was most likely a *viola da gamba* of the cello range (most often with a low note *D*), while the latter might be a long bass lute called a *theorbo*, or a *harpsichord*, or an *organ*. The harmonic member of the *basso continuo* duplicated the bass melody, or most of it, and furnished the chord structures of the harmonic element in the middle register. The modernity was emphasized by absence of middle lines in the polyphonic sense, and the specific omission of the tenor, which had been the structural spine of polyphony and the focus of attention of the listener, must have created an astonishing effect.

The notation of the basso continuo thus comprised a twofold system of a melody plus a series of signs indicating the desired harmony (mostly numbers indicating intervals above the bass, but also sharp and flat signs—the natural sign was not generally used until the last part of the century— dashes, and slashes). This was called a *figured bass*; it required two players, one to play the melody and one to *realize* the harmony.

MONODIC MUSIC

Monody was being performed in several Italian centers at the turn of the century.

In Florence, a group of intellectuals was meeting at the court of Count Bardi, calling themselves the *Camerata* (club or camaraderie). The members of the Camerata included Giulio Caccini (c. 1546-1618), who was the Count's secretary for over a quarter of a century. He was renowned as a singer and was an early practitioner of monody, writing and singing solo madrigals in the new style during the last decade of the sixteenth century. He brought out a group of them in 1602; the publication used the figured bass and also included a preface explaining the aims of the style. He called his book *Le Nuove Musiche* (The New Music). In addition, Caccini, in collaboration with Jacopo Peri (1561-1633), another Camerata member, composed a *dramma per musica* (drama in or through music), a version of the popular myth of Orpheus and Euridice, called *Euridice* and produced in 1600 as part of the wedding festival of France's Henry IV and Marie de Medici.

In Rome in 1600, Emilio del Cavalieri (c. 1550-1602), an aristocrat acquainted with the Camerata, produced another type of monodic drama, a religious allegory called *La rappresentazione di anima e di corpo*. (A *rappresentazione* was a theatrical representation, while *anima* and *corpo* mean "soul" and "body"—because of its theatrical nature, monody was also called the *stilo rappresentativo*.) This work was produced at the Roman oratory of St. Philip Neri (1515-1595), devoted to popular religious music, and it used some of the materials of the early *laude*, popular religious songs of praise.

In Mantua, the cathedral music director Lodovico Grossi de Viadana (1564-1645) was experimenting with sacred music in the new style. He combined voices and instruments in a new spirit of exploiting contrasts called *stilo concertato* to create a type of musical work which he called a *concerto*, a word meaning both "competing" and "accommodating." In 1602 he published *Cento concerti ecclesiastici* (One Hundred Church Concertos).

It was in Mantua and Venice that the greatest exponent of the new style produced many of his works. Claudio Monteverdi (1567-1643), one of the towering figures in the history of music, explored the new style in four books of madrigals (1605 to 1638—four earlier books had been in the old style). These included madrigals for two tenors and basso continuo, an expansion of the treble-and-bass polarity to a two-trebles-and-bass texture, the two functions of the bass balanced by the twofold top lines. He also used the new style in sacred music, such as his setting of the entire music for *Vespers* (1610), and finally, he produced a series of operas still in the repertoire. The new did not displace the old for Monteverdi, who used plainchant tenors in the *Vespers* and combined consorts to form the instrumental component of his earliest opera *Orfeo* (Mantua, 1607). The *Lamento* (a formalized mourning song with a heritage older than the troubadours) from his opera *Arianna* (1608), which had survived through its separate publication (the opera score is lost), was popular long into the century. His late masterpiece *L'incoronazione di Poppea* (The Coronation of Poppea, Venice 1642) was more exclusively in the *stilo rappresentativo*; essentially declamatory rather than melodic, it achieved an emotional and dramatic validity of amazing depth and scope.

Plate II

A. Viola da gamba. Plate XX of the second volume of *Syntagma Musicum* (1618) by Michael Praetorius.

1, 2, and 3 are treble, tenor, and bass viole da gamba, all played on the leg.   4 is a viola bastarda, which the English called the lyra viol and considered the perfect continuo instrument. Praetorius described it as "a kind of viola da gamba, . . . [with a] body somewhat longer and larger than that of the tenor."   5 is a lyra da braccio, played on the arm; it was already on the decline. A century earlier, it had been the instrument of Leonardo da Vinci, who was said by a friend to be a "divine improviser" on that instrument.

Plate II—*Continued*

B. Gentleman playing a viola da gamba. Illustration from *The Division-Viol, or The Art of Playing Ex Tempore Upon a Ground*, (1659), by Christopher Simpson.

This engraving illustrated correct technique, the instrument resting on the calves of the legs, the bow held palm up. In the second edition (1667) the gentleman's hat, being out of fashion, was removed.

Example 1

A. *Aria Terza* (Third Air or Song) from *Le Nuove Musiche* (1602) by Giulio Caccini. Facsimile of the original edition.

The notation is on two staves, using a second-line G clef (treble) and a third-line F clef (baritone). In the baritone clef, both upper and lower B's are flatted in the signature.

The bass is figured, with the absence of figures in the first measure and a half an indication of the presence of a fifth and a third over each essential bass note (in this case, half- and quarter-notes); the figures represent intervals other than 5 and 3 above the bass; the 6 over d in Measure 2, for example, changes 5 to 6 but does not affect 3, making the chord d-f-$b\flat$; 11 and $\sharp$10 over d are g^1 and $f\sharp^1$ (an octave plus a fourth and third, the latter to be altered by a sharp-sign), these changing 3 but leaving 5 unaffected, making the chord d-a-g^1 followed by d-a-f $\sharp^1$.

The original was printed in movable type, each symbol on a separate bit of metal, along with its bit of staff; this procedure was satisfactory as long as only one note at a time was used on each staff. The staff lines are actually made up of a series of segments, giving them an unsteadiness characteristic

Example 1—*Continued*

of that technique. The sign ⁓ at the end of the staves served as a guide to the first note of the next line; this sign was called a custos (from the Greek *kystos*, guardian).

B. *Aria Terza* from *Le Nuove Musiche* (1602) by Giulio Caccini. Transcription into modern notation.

The flat sign above e^2 (in Measure 2) is an editor's indication that the note is to be sung flat, but that the flat sign is not in the original. Such alterations were assumed in the tradition of the day, and are now standard editorial practice in modern publications.

The runs toward the end of the vocal part are decorative, and their rhythmic indication is not to be taken literally. Such an embellishment was called a *tirata*, or rip (the word means "torn" or "ripped"), in French a *tirade*. The *tirata* was one of the most popular of embellishments of the Baroque, and *tirate* are found through the Classical style as well.

The next to last note of the solo voice, a step above the final tone, was generally embellished with rhythmic articulation or a trill.

By the middle of the seventeenth century, Italian opera was established in public opera houses as well as in court theatres—the first, San Cassiano in Venice, opened in 1637. The action of the operas was carried out in monodic vocal music, now called *recitativo*, interspersed with songs or *arias*. The recitativo was the main texture of early opera; it was declaimed in a free style (though written in a meter), without an overall tonal center. The aria had a tonal center and a meter, and was generally in a *da capo* form: a primary section, or aria, A, a contrasting section, B, followed by instructions to repeat the *aria da capo* (from the beginning). *Recitativo* dominated opera in the first half of the century, but by the early eighteenth century, the aria took over the primary position. Complaints of "the tedium of the recitative" in the early years changed to later complaints about the domination of the aria, which was highly embellished by the glamorous singing stars who were the rage of Europe.

SUGGESTIONS FOR FURTHER STUDY

Records

Recordings of early monody are rare and tend to be disappointing. The Monteverdi *Orfeo*, Archive, ARC—3035/6, for example, is slow and suggests little of the excitement of the original.

RECOMMENDED

MONTEVERDI, *Vespro della Beata Vergine* (1610) by the Concentus Musicus of Vienna. Telefunken (S) 9501/2.

400th Anniversary Album: Claudio Monteverdi, Scherzi Musicale Project Records, PR 7001 SD.

Solo Airs, Spiritual Song, and Theatrical Spectacle

INTERNATIONAL TYPES

olo song and theatrical spectacle comprised the international music of the first half of the seventeenth century. These were both well established in Renaissance music, though in the early years of the seventeenth century they tended to expand their reach to the growing middle classes. The monodic style came slowly out of Italy, meeting the national forms in various stages of growth and development.

ENGLAND

In England the *lute song* and the court *masque* were at their height in the first years of the seventeenth century. Although emulation of Italian style (in many aspects of culture) was rampant, and the vogue for the *madrigal* had been an Italian importation of the last dozen years of the sixteenth century, the lute song at the hands of such consummate artists as John Dowland (1563-1626) was a truly British art. The great poets at the turn of the century included William Shakespeare (1564-1616); their poetry made full use of a language of many derivations, unprecedented scope of allusion, and unique power. Dowland was a poet, composer, singer, and lutenist—the kind of artist who can appear only at moments of cultural climax. England under Elizabeth I and James I presented such a moment.

The court masque was loosely organized and theatrical, most generally an extended allegory of poems, songs, and dances joined with stage effects (produced with complex machinery) and elaborate cos-

Example 2

A. "Shall I Sue," a lute song from the *Second Booke of Songes or Ayres* (1600) by John Dowland.

2 Silly wretch forfake thefe dreames,
    of a vaine defire,
O bethinke what hie regard,
    holy hopes doe require.
Fauour is as faire as things are,
    treafure is not bought,
Fauour is not wonne with words,
    nor the wifh of a thought.

3 Pittie is but a poore defence,
    for a dying hart,
Ladies eies refpe& no mone,
    in a meane defert.
Shee is to worthie far,
    for a worth fo bafe,
Cruell and but iuft is fhee,
    in my iuft difgrace.

Iuftice giues each man his owne,
    though my loue bee iuft,
Yet will not fhee pittie my griefe,
    therefore die I muft,
Silly hart then yeeld to die,
    perifh in difpaire,
Witneffe yet how faine I die,
    When I die for the faire.

Example 2—*Continued*

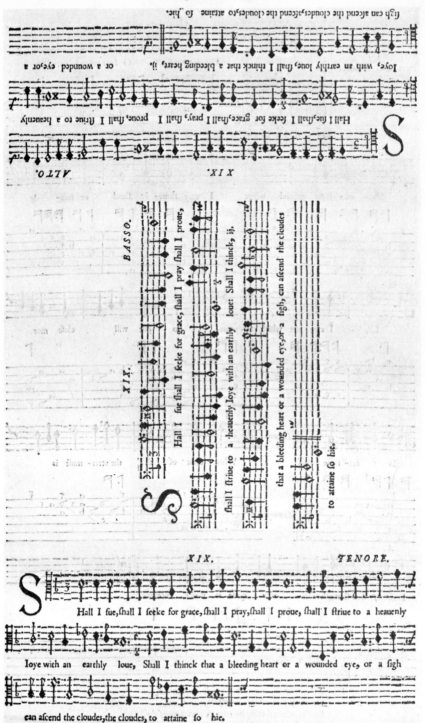

Example 2—*Continued*

Shall I sue, shall I seeke for grace, shall I pray, shall I prove,

Shall I strive to a heaven - ly Ioy, with an earth - ly love?

Shall I think that a bleed - ing hart or a wound-ed eie,

Or a sigh can as-cend the cloudes to at - taine so hie.

The lute part has a variable number of separate lines, and the leading of one note to another is largely left to the performer (though this aspect of performance is suggested in the modern notation). The original was printed in lute tablature, in which what appear to be staff lines actually represent strings of the long lute or theorbo. The strings, from top to bottom, are g^1, d^1, a, f, c, G; a letter on a line means that the string it represents is to be plucked, with the particular letter indicating hand position—a for the open string, b for the first fret, c for the second fret, and so forth. The opening chord, for example, indicates open g^1 and d^1 with the letter a on those strings, while the third string, f, is figured with the letter c for the second fret, producing two half-steps above the open sound, or g. Letters below the staff refer to the added, unstopped strings of the theorbo; these were variously tuned. Both tuning and the details of tablature varied from country to country.

The song is complete on the left-hand page of the original; additional parts are given on the right for polyphonic performance. Placement of the book on a small table allows for sitting at different angles, alto opposite tenor, with bass at the side. In the polyphonic tradition, the voice parts of the polyphonic version proceeds with rhythmic freedom without the need of measure bars. The sign $\mathfrak{z}$ is a repeat sign; the last two lines of the modern version are to be repeated in performance—the sign comes in the middle of the original. Such a format offered options for performance: voices in polyphony, a solo voice with lute (one or two persons), or both.

By indicating precise pitches, tablature editions help historians to clarify the practice of *musica ficta*, the introduction and maintenance of chromatic alterations, which were determined in earlier practice without consistent indication in the notation.

The printing technique is mixed—the tablature is engraved and the vocal parts are printed from movable type. The engraving plates were so heavy that the impressions can be seen from the opposite sides of the pages.

tumes to produce a splendid and extravagant entertainment. The masque was the single extended English entertainment of the first years of the seventeenth century. The composer Henry Lawes (1595-1662) composed the masque *Comus* (1633) to a text by the poet John Milton (1608-1674); it was known particularly for its accommodating the English tongue to the new ideas of musical declamation. English music suffered a long break during the Commonwealth. King Charles I was beheaded in 1649, and the government was in the hands of conservatives, who frowned upon public entertainment, until the Restoration, the accession of Charles II in 1660. Like most composers, Lawes went into semiretired private employ during the Commonwealth, but he had already published Psalm paraphrases for solo voice and thoroughbass (1637) and during the interregnum he produced three volumes of *Ayres and Dialogues for 1, 2, and 3 Voices* (1653, 1655, 1658) which maintained his reputation. It was Lawes who composed the Coronation Anthem for Charles II in 1660.

Example 3

"Ah me too many Deaths," a song from *Orpheus Britannicus* (1698) by Henry Purcell.

Example 3—*Continued*

II

Ah me! to many Deaths decreed,
By Love or War, I hourly dye,
When I see not my love I bleed;
Yet when I have him in my Eye,
He kills me with excess of Joy.

By now the person realizing the figured bass had to decide on exact spacing of the rhythmic motion indicated by the figures; the 7–6 in Measure 3 might be two quarter-notes, but might be a dotted-quarter and eighth, or even a free, unmeasured progression. The performer also had to decide which bass tones were essential, requiring separate chords, and which were unessential, to be treated as passing tones. The eighth-notes of Measure 22, for example, each might well have a separate chord structure, but the sixteenth-notes of Measure 21 include passing tones.

The four-beat measure is made of two virtually equal half-measures of two beats each; comparison of the passages beginning at Measure 22 and at the mid-point of Measure 24 will show that the composer felt that both strong beats and both weak beats were interchangeable. It will also show that the last five measures contain two phrases of two and a half measures each. Such a view of the four-beat measure persisted through the Baroque and beyond.

After the Restoration, the court masque prospered again; in solo song, the basso continuo had won out over the lute. Matthew Locke (c. 1632-1677) published the first text on the new style in English: *Melathesia, or Certain General Rules for Playing Upon a Continued Bass* (1673). John Blow (1649-1708), an organist and choirmaster who held posts at the Royal Chapel from 1660 and also at Westminster Abbey and St. Paul's Cathedral, was less of a modernist, but his *Amphion Anglicus* (1700), a collection of fifty English Songs, was in the new style. His *Masque for the Entertainment of the King: Venus and Adonis* (1684) was one of the great masques.

Henry Purcell (c. 1659-1695), perhaps the greatest native composer of English musical history, wrote music for some fifty theatrical productions, in some cases just a song or two, but in others a complete musical score. His most famous theatre work was *Dido and Æneas,* composed about 1689 in the tradition of the masque but generally considered an opera because of its sustained action. In addition, he wrote a large number of songs which were collected after his death and published as the *Orpheus Britannicus* (1698), for one, two, and three voices with thoroughbass. Many of these songs have never left the repertoire.

FRANCE

In France the court song (*air de cour*) and ballet dominated the first three quarters of the seventeenth century. The main types of French song were the lute song to a formal poem (*air sérieux*), a convivial or drinking song (*air à boire*), the song to religious text (*chanson spirituel*), monody (*récit chanté*) and accompanied solo song (*chanson à voix seule*). The many collections of the lutenist-singer Etienne Moulinié (at court from about 1620 to about 1660) included all categories. The most famous of composers of *airs de cour* was Antoine Boesset (1586-1643), whose songs were among the most popular of the century. Caccini had visited the French court between 1601 and 1605, but in spite of the French acquaintance with the *stile nuovo*, the use of the *basso continuo* did not take hold in France until later in the century. The lute was so popular that the lute song, for vocal solo and accompaniment, remained the staple even in the *récit chanté*.

The French *air de cour* was the basis of the court spectacle, the *ballet de cour*, in the first half of the century. Over two hundred *ballets de cour* were produced in France by 1643, when the five-year-old Louis XIV acceded to the throne of France. The reign of Louis XIII (1610-1643) and the years of the youth of Louis XIV comprised the heyday of the lavish ballet in France. Louis XIV was a fine dancer and starred in many productions from 1651 to 1669. Moulinié had also been a good

Plate III

The Lute Player. Painting by Orazio Gentileschi (c. 1565-1639).

The painting shows the lute's ribbed, rounded back, which made the instrument difficult to hold. It was generally placed on a table or on the player's knee, raised by placing his foot on a step or stool. A violin, with its bow, lies on the table, along with a wind instrument and two books of music.

National Gallery of Art, Washington, D. C. Ailsa Mellon Bruce Fund. With permission.

dancer. The French danced to spoken poetry, to song, and to instrumental dances, but the *air de cour* formed the largest dance literature, and the great lutenists were dancers as well as singers and composers.

The *ballet de cour* was a spectacle of costume, poetry, song, dance, and stage effects. According to a late sixteenth-century producer of ballets, the form was a true synthesis of the arts, "combining several rare and rich adornments, I can say with pleasure, into a well-proportioned work [for] the eye, the ear, and the understanding."[1]

Music for the ballet was of two basic types: the *récit chanté*, a musical declamation of a poetic text, in a free—verbal—rhythm and the *air mesurée*, or measured tune. Subjects included allegorical, mythological, political, and comic types. The music included chorus and instrumental chamber music as well as *récits chantés* and *airs mesurées*; in the *Ballet de l'Adventure de Tancrède en la forest enchantée* (1619), the mythological plot was furthered by machines, through which "the heavens parted in two, and within, there appeared the King's Chapel music, consisting of thirty musicians all suspended in the aforesaid Heavens, and this music sang a dialogue with that of the Chamber."[2]

The last master of the *ballet de cour* was the Italian-born composer-producer Jean-Baptiste Lully (1632-1687), whose long career in the service of the young Louis XIV saw the switch from the instrumental domination of the lute to the basic string choir with *basse continue*, and the switch from the title *ballet* to *opéra*, a spectacle defined by the presence of *récitative*, or declamation imported from the Italian monody. The French extravaganza was changed, but not in essence; the opera could sustain as lavish a staging as the ballet, but could sustain a longer and more complex plot. Louis XIV in his forties and fifties became the foremost royal patron of opera, and Lully's works formed the basis of the French opera of the seventeenth century.

Lully had been a violinist and dancer, and had been a companion to his young monarch; he directed the band of violinists, violists, and cellists called *Les 24 Violons du Roi* (The 24 Violins of the King), and a smaller chamber contingent called *Les Petits Violons* (the Little [group of] Violins). His contributions lay in the development of a style of *récitative* suited to the French tongue, and in the expansion of instrumental techniques and forms in opera. The French overture, a slow-fast-slow format with a characteristic dotted figure in the majestic opening slow section, was an important contribution to instrumental forms; the use of flutes, oboes, bassoons, horns, trumpets, and kettle-drums in the opera orchestra was an important contribution to instrumental technique.

---

[1]Beaujoyeulx, in the preface to *Le Balet Comique de la Royne*, 1581. Quoted by André Verchaly, in "Air de Cour, Ballet de Cour," *Historie de la Musique*. 2 vols., *Encyclopédie de la Pléiade* (Paris: Gallimard, 1960), 1, 1549.
[2]*Ibid.*, I, 1552.

Lully's recitative differed from the Italian in being more melodic, with less distinction between *récitative* and *air*, and by accommodating to the stressless French by constant change of meter. The comparison of Italian and French styles was the subject of much impassioned argument throughout the whole of the rest of the seventeenth and eighteenth centuries, and the continuing disputation was given the name "the war of the French and Italian taste." Unlike England and Germany, both of whom capitulated to the Italian taste by the end of the Baroque, France retained a national style. It was characterized by the French love of the dance and of motivating rhythms deriving from the dance, and by the French delight in instrumental color, for which they have been known not only in the Baroque era but through the Romantic period as well.

GERMANY

In the German states, the introduction of the new style was strongly linked to religious music. The devastation of the Thirty Years' War (1618-1648) left some three hundred small states—each with a city or court center. Primary to the rebuilding of the German states was the establishment of the Protestant churches, which became the civic centers of culture and education. The *Cantor*, a church music director and teacher (and most often a composer as well), was the crucial musician of the German states after the Thirty Years' War.

The pervading figure of German music in the first half of the seventeenth century was Heinrich Schütz, also called Sagitarius, (1585-1672), a man of long creative power, one of the great lifelong modernists of the history of Western music, and one of the most influential in the dissemination of the new style. He had studied music and law in Germany; then, from 1609 to 1612, he worked in Venice, studying with Giovanni Gabrieli. His works included Italian madrigals (published in 1611), polyphonic Psalms for double choir (1619), *Cantiones Sacræ* (Sacred Songs, 1625), an opera, *Dafne* (1627—lost), *Geistliche Konzerte* (Spiritual Concertos, 1636-1639), and three volumes of *Symphoniae Sacræ* (Sacred Symphonies 1629, 1647, 1650). He worked in Dresden and Copenhagen, among other centers, moving frequently and exerting his influence widely, even during the war years. He was, like Monteverdi, a man of the transition. His choral works, which comprise a significant part of his total, combined old and new styles.

In a sense, so did the sacred concertos of Johann Hermann Schein (1586-1630), whose *Opella nova*, sixty-two concertos in two volumes (1618 and 1626), were settings of German Protestant hymn tunes (*chorales*). The *Christ lag in Todesbanden* (Christ lay in the Bonds of

Example 4

Sacred Concerto from *Opella Nova* (1618) by Schein. Opening two lines of the chorale text. The note values have been cut to their modern equivalents (𝅗𝅥 to ♩).

Example 4—*Continued*

Death), an Easter hymn by Martin Luther, was set typically in the earlier volume, combining two treble parts (Cantus I and II) and a tenor with a basso continuo. In the chorale the two treble lines were set off, with the bass, in an elaborate three-part polar texture using quarter- and eighth-notes, while the tenor stated the chorale in steady half-notes, generally in alternation with the two treble lines, combining with them at the second and fourth lines (of six) of the hymn, and in a final alleluia section of four phrases or *puncti*. The original combined new and old: the polar texture and basso continuo of the new plus the tenor cantus firmus of the old; the new ideas of chorale elaboration with the old punctus structure, in particular the imitative point; and, in notation, the figured bass with measure bars, along with the upper parts in the old style, as polyphonic lines, printed separately, without bar lines.

Schein was the Cantor of St. Thomas Church in Leipzig from 1616 to his death in 1630, and, like most of the important Germans of the century, was primarily associated with sacred music, both through the concertos and a collection of 312 sacred songs and Psalms in German and Latin and in both old and new style, published in 1627 as the *Augsburgischer Konfession* and reissued in a new edition in 1645. (See Example 10, page 91.) He also contributed to the popular music literature, notably with a collection of dances, the *Banchetto musicale* (1617).

Another important contribution to German *Lied* (song), both sacred and secular, lay in the *Arien* (airs) of Adam Krieger (1634-1666), which established the solo song as a rich German art.

The inventiveness of the Germans in sacred concertos and in song did not extend to the operatic stages. The war and the divisions of the German states left many small courts instead of the great French one, several small struggling city-states instead of the few wealthy Italian ones. It was too late for German composers to begin a native operatic art; singers were not available and it was easier to import Italian singers than to train German ones in an art inimical to the German training schools, which were in the churches. Opera was an Italian import in Germany for some fifty years after the war. Just at the end of the seventeenth century, a brilliant school of German opera was formed in the city of Hamburg under the German Reinhard Keiser (1674-1739), who was co-director from 1703; he composed 116 operas on German texts (of which fewer than 20 have been found). But other cities remained Italian in operatic loyalty, and when Keiser left the Hamburg opera, that city returned to the Italian art as well. At the end of the Baroque era only France had a strong tradition of opera in her native tongue.

SUGGESTIONS FOR FURTHER STUDY

Records

German and Latin Sacred Songs and Psalms. Lyrichord: (7) 146.

Louis XIII Roi de France: Ballet de la Merlaison (1635). Nonesuch H-71130.

Schein: 3 Suites from "Banchetto Musicale" (1617) Archive ARC 3153.

A selection of Purcell works, including secular songs sung by the countertenor Alfred Deller, is on the two-record album of vocal and instrumental items. Bach (70) 570/1.

Books and Music

HOLLAND, A. K. *Henry Purcell, The English Musical Tradition* Penguin Books, #679, 1948.

MITFORD, NANCY. *The Sun King* New York: Harper & Row, Publishers, 1966.

PURCELL, HENRY. *Orpheus Britannicus.* A facsimile of the edition of 1698. New York: Broude Brothers, 1965.

SCHEIN, JOHANN HERMANN. *Sacred Concerto* from *Opella Nova*—New York: Alexander Broude, Tetra Choral Series (Octavo separate for choir and organ) AB 225-10; edited by Kurt Stone. 1968.

New Types
of
Music for Voice

A NEW IDEAL OF MELODY

he monodic fabric gave special focus to the solo part with a concentration upon its particular line and emotional thrust not possible in a polyphonic fabric. The separation of function of treble and bass, which gave harmonic responsibility to the basso continuo, opened the treble for exploration of the solo. Coupled with the theatrical experiments of the Camerata, the new concept of melody had become *recitative*, a musical declamation of dramatic texts, generally in a free style without repetition, and in a phrase structure deriving its overall form almost completely from the words. Although this proved ideal in the *dramma per musica* in carrying on intense dramatic verbal action, it was unsatisfactory as a musical constant, since a musical work seeks a musical form in addition to a verbal one. Thus the song—air, aria, Lied, chanson—soon came to have equal importance with recitative as its complement and balance, so that at the height of the Baroque—at the end of the seventeenth century—the two flourished side by side.

One element of melodic form is repetition of rhythm or contour pattern; in Baroque music this took the form of the *subject*, a characteristic combination of rhythmic figure and linear shape that formed the basic melodic idea of the era. The ideal of performance was clarity— a separate impetus for each tone, with accuracy of rhythm and intonation the prime element of melodic vitality.

TONE QUALITY: VOICE AND VIOLIN

The vocal ideal was of the high voice, the countertenor, and the soprano, both the female and male. In England, where voices change typically at seventeen or eighteen, the boy soprano voice has always been beloved. In Italy, where the change is typically at twelve or thirteen, it was customary to castrate the most gifted boys before their change of voice—at the peak of the practice some four thousand boys per year—in order to maintain the soprano range. The *castrato* had the barrel chest of the eunuch, with magnificent wind supply and control, yet maintained the register of a woman.

Italy was alone in perpetrating the *castrato*, in the medical sense, but these singers were supported with huge fees and matching adulation everywhere in Europe and the British Isles. The rage of the castrato was a defining aspect of the Baroque musical art.

The violin was the instrumental counterpart of the soprano voice, and that instrument reached its maturity in the hands of the great Baroque makers and performers. It was a modern instrument, displayed in Baroque *gabinetti* (cabinets—private museums) alongside such other modern instruments as the microscope. It emulated the voice in its technique of clear, delineated tone production, and also in its expression of moods, called the *Passions*. These were many, but centered in two chief styles: the *allegro* (in French *gai*) mood, characterized by disjunct motion, short notes, and diatonic scale materials; and the *adagio* (in French *lent*), characterized by conjunct motion, long notes, and chromatic scale materials. The first required clarity of attack, with notes clearly disconnected and highly energized; the second called for sustained tone, frequent slurs (though not a continuous legato), and a greater number of added embellishments.

> Embellishments are to the Voice and to the Instruments what Ornaments are to an Edifice. . . . When the Voice uses them perfectly, it is this model that Instruments should emulate.[3]

Vocal technique of the seventeenth century was called *bel canto*, beautiful singing. The singers sang with great dexterity and grace, which they sought above loudness or fullness of tone; vibrato was one of the embellishments, and deftness was prized, along with purity. The violin ideal was the same. Both violinist and singer prized *bravura*, or technical display, and treasured the skill of the *fioratura*, or ornate "passage." The *cadenza*, or freely embellished cadence, which demanded both technical skill and the mastery of the *Passions*, along with imagination, was the summit of their art.

---

[3]Jean Rousseau, *Traité de la viole* (1687), facsimile edition. (Amsterdam: Antiqua, 1965), p. 74.

Courtesy of the Stellfeld Purchase, The University of Michigan Library, Ann Arbor.
Photo by R. E. Kalmbach.

THE CANTATA IN ITALY

At the middle of the seventeenth century, the vocal-instrumental music of the new style was called the *cantata,* referring to its being sung. The cantata had begun as a monodic work, generally for solo voice and basso continuo. Some were very close to continuous *recitativo,* sounding very much like excerpts from *dramme per musica;* but the texts tended less to theatricality, and more often the style had resembled song in a monodic type described as *arioso,* song-like. But gradually the general, free arioso gave way in both directions, and passages of *recitativo* and *arioso* were interspersed with song (*aria*), generally in the *ABA* form with only *AB* written out and the *da capo* indication to repeat *A* from the beginning—a repetition which gave the singer a fine opportunity to improvise embellishment and variation.

Luigi Rossi (1598-1653), who spent six years in Florence but worked mainly in Rome, was an important composer of the period defining the cantata. Over 375 of his works remain, virtually all of them vocal. He himself was a guitarist, organist, and harpsichordist as well as a composer-producer, yet it was as a singer that he was most famous. (He was called "the new swan.") His operas were important as well; he produced his *Orfeo* in Paris in 1647, introducing monody to that capitol.

Alessandro Stradella (1642-1682), a singer and composer from Naples, contributed to both opera and cantata with works performed in Venice and Rome, popular from England and France to Germany and Austria.

The Sicilian Alessandro Scarlatti (1660-1725), who worked in Rome and, more importantly in Naples, became the chief figure in the Neapolitan opera, turning Naples into an operatic center not only of Italy, but of all Europe. His 115 operas only suggest his creative drive; well

---

Plate IV

Lady at a keyboard. Early seventeenth-century engraving showing a table clavichord, typical of continental instruments, in contrast to the similar table harpsichord, the *virginals,* in use in England. This instrument is evidently a fretted clavichord, one in which more than one pitch could be obtained on one string. On the clavichord, the *tangent,* the small metal blade that touched the string upon depression of the key, remained on the string, whose sounding length was thus measured from the bridge to the tangent, a unique feature of the clavichord. Two adjacent keys, whose pitches were close and unlikely to be sounded together, could thus be served by a single string, by having the tangents strike the string at two places to create the two pitches. The difference of a semitone on a clavichord string was approximately the same length as on a lute, whose frets measured off the semitones.

Example 5

Recitativo and Aria from the solo cantata *Rispetto e Amore* (c. 1695) by Alessandro Scarlatti. Facsimile of a contemporary manuscript, possibly Scarlatti's own, housed at the University of Michigan Library.

Example 5—*Continued*

Courtesy of the Stellfeld Purchase, The University of Michigan Library, Ann Arbor.
Photo by R. E. Kalmbach.

The two parts are written on a first-line *C* clef (soprano) and a fourth line *F* clef (bass). Where the text interferes, the figures of the bass are below rather than above the bass part. The first bass note is *g*, the second is *e*, figured *6*. The soprano solo begins with a downward skip from d^2 to b^1.

The recitativo (marked Re^o) begins in the declamatory style and ends as arioso. It cadences to an A major triad (a sharp above and slightly to the left of the final bass tone raises the third), which serves as dominant to the ensuing Aria; the end of the recitativo is marked "*Sub.*" (for *subito*, suddenly), a standard indication to proceed without pause.

The Aria is in *d* minor (without a signature, also standard); it is marked *Aria* and (under the bass) and^{te} (for *andante*), a walking beat, in this case with two beats to the measure, as indicated by the meter signature. The flat sign on *c* in the bass (Measure 6) cancels the sharp just preceding; the flat sign meant not to put a flat-sign in front of the note, but to *flatten* it, lower it a half tone below the possible or specified pitch. The end of the Aria proper is marked with a double bar; the contrasting section follows and is actually the final section to be notated. The last indication is the *Da Capo*, at the end of the final score. Beneath, the word *Fine* (end) indicates the end of the entire cantata.

---

over a thousand cantatas have already been found (and many more are thought to exist). His cantatas represent the apex of that form in Italy. They were based on alternating *recitativo* and aria, generally two pairs (four sections). The recitativo was free, either dramatic or arioso; the difference lay basically in the spare chordal underpinnings and straightforward vocal lines of the first as contrasted with the relatively active bass and more melodic solo line in the second. In either case it was set off as a type from the aria, which was in a key, and was conceived in terms of melodic subjects as characterized by metric regularity and distinctive contour.

Scarlatti's cantatas included duets (for two singers—typically two sopranos—and basso continuo), cantatas for soloist and solo instrument (flute or violin) with basso continuo, and, rarely, cantatas with a larger contingent of instruments or a choir. But over three-quarters of his cantatas were for solo voice and basso continuo, and the great bulk were in a four-section format of recitativo-aria-recitativo-aria. Although it should not be considered the only type of cantata, it is this small group, one singer and two instrumentalists—most likely viola da gamba and harpsichord—for the continuo, and the four-section format, which represents the Italian cantata of the Baroque.

THE CANTATA IN OTHER COUNTRIES

In Italy, the cantata was the standard vocal concert piece from the middle of the seventeenth century, performed in the main hall or chamber (*camera*) at court; its texts were in Italian and generally allegorical or mythological in keeping with formal entertainments. In France, the cantata (in French *cantate*) was introduced about 1700, and it took on the same character of *salon* entertainment. The term *cantate* remained with the court entertainment, which grew larger until in the lesser courts the cantate became an evening's luxurious production, with scenery and costumes—much less than an opera but much more than the *cantate* had originally been. The most famous of these were the cantatas of Jean Joseph Mouret (1682-1739), famous singer and composer who worked at Sceaux, the palace of the Duc du Maine, the favorite (illegitimate) son of Louis XIV; his cantatas were published as *Les Grandes Nuits de Sceaux* (The Grand Nights of Sceaux). The French used the term *cantatille* for the four-movement concert cantatas at the end of the Baroque. Like the Italians, the French preferred mythological and allegorical texts and defined the type as being in their native tongue.

In addition, the French cultivated the same form with sacred Latin text, a solo or duet work called the *petit motet* (small motet, in contrast to the larger choral form); these developed after the institution of the *Concert spirituel*, a Paris public concert series using the personnel of the national opera and producing "spiritual concerts"—i.e., music with sacred text or without text, in the manner of the older *ecclesiastical concerto* and *sacred symphony*. The *petits motets* of Mouret were a staple of the *Concert spirituel* for a generation.

In England, the cantata before 1700 was an extended song—several of Purcell's were included in the *Orpheus Britannicus*, including the famous *Bess of Bedlam*, often called *Mad Bess*, which was still being featured on English concerts in the nineteenth century. But after 1700, the concert singers were either Italians or English singers who had studied in Italy, and the Italian cantata became standard, either imported Italian examples or works written in the Italian style to Italian texts.

In Germany, the cantata was put to the service of the Protestant church as the *anthem* was in England. German Cantors used the forces at hand: the church organ, from which they conducted and which provided the harmonic aspect of the continuo; singers, including soloists and choir attached to the church as regulars or apprentices. The apprentices were students learning to be professional musicians (not necessarily of the church), studying a variety of instruments, which meant that instrumental teachers and students were also at hand. In addition, the apprentices provided a ready corps of music copyists to prepare new scores and parts, making new works easy and inexpensive to produce.

Typically, the German cantata was an extension of the *geistliche Lieder* (sacred songs) and the Italian cantata, a work for soloists, choir, organ, and instruments; it was often composed on a chorale or a sacred song, probably with a text suited to the particular Sunday or Holy Day on which it was sung. The early German cantatas were the works of such men as Dietrich Buxtehude (1637-1707) and Johann Pachelbel (1653-1706), in which chorales, solo and duet arias, were combined with extended choral movements. The chorales were harmonized hymn tunes, akin to the old familiar style, while the choruses were akin to the learned style, using the imitative point as well as simpler textures. Often the result was international; some cantatas used recitative, some used arias in the Italian style; the chorales themselves were Germanic, while the choruses tended to conservative grandness. The German cantata culminated in the first half of the eighteenth century with the two hundred cantatas of Johann Sebastian Bach (1685-1750), the Cantor at St. Thomas Church in Leipzig from 1723—a hundred years after Schein's sacred concertos had been heard there.

LARGE CHORAL WORKS

In Italy and later in Germany and England, the chief large choral form of the Baroque era was the *oratorio*, named for the *oratory*, founded in Rome by St. Philip Neri late sixteenth century, where religious songs and allegories in the popular style were produced. By the middle of the seventeenth century, a long concert work telling a Biblical tale had been developed by such composers as Giacomo Carissimi (1605-1674), an organist and teacher in Rome, renowned as the leading composer of the new sacred stories. He put the recitative into the central job of narration, using soloists for direct quotation and a choir for groups, as the story line suggested, with instrumental interludes to suggest scenes such as a battle, a storm, or a period of sleep—all of which became set pieces and were much in vogue by the end of the century. The central role was that of the narrator or *historicus* (sometimes called the *testo*, Italian for "text"), who sang in recitative, but as the form developed, solo and choral movements increased in size and importance.

In Italy, the oratorio was the characteristic large choral form, along with settings of the large sacred texts, such as the *Gloria*, the *Magnificat*, and, after 1729 when it was reintroduced to the liturgy, the *Stabat Mater*. Giovanni Battista Pergolesi (1710-1736) and Antonio Vivaldi (1669?-1741) were two Italian masters known for such large works. In England, the oratorio flourished in Italian works by the German-born, English-naturalized composer George Frideric Handel (1685-1759), who brought both Italian opera and oratorio to a high vogue in Great Britain. But his most famous work was an oratorio *Messiah*, on an arrangement of Old and New Testament texts, in English, which was premiered in Dublin in 1742.

In Germany, the great works were oratorios dealing with the story of the Crucifixion, called the *Passion*. Settings of the story in the versions of the various Gospels were extremely popular. Schütz had been the first German oratorio composer, with his *Historia der Geburt Jesu Christi* (Story of the Birth of Jesus Christ, called the *Christmas Oratorio*, 1664), three *Passions*, and a German *Magnificat*. It was little over a half century before Bach was fulfilling the form in his giant *Passions* according to St. John and St. Matthew, the *Magnificat*, and the great concert setting of the Latin Mass texts, the *Missa in H-moll*, the B minor Mass.

In France the characteristic choral work was the *motet à grand chœur* (motet for full choir), or *grand motet*, a work to a Latin sacred text without a story, most often a Psalm. In the time of Louis XIV, a *grand motet* was performed during Low Mass at the Chapel of Versailles, celebrated daily at 10:00 A.M. The composer Michel-Richard de Lalande (or Delalande, 1657-1726) was the early master of these works; 72 remain, and some of them were published posthumously by his widow. Jean-Joseph Cassanéa de Mondonville (1711-1772) was the later master of the grand motet; he was a musician of Louis XV, who had discontinued the morning Chapel Mass as practiced by his predecessor. Mondonville wrote for the *Concert spirituel,* where his motets were standard program finales from 1740 until the French Revolution.

All of the large choral works—oratorio, Passion, grand motet, and even the larger German cantata—were based upon the same general principles of construction: each verse became a separate movement—a recitative, solo, duet, orchestral interlude, or chorus—in an alternation of types. National variations were brought about naturally: the historicus appeared in the oratorio but not the *grand motet;* French choir types —the full chorus of five parts, and the solo choir of three or four voices and seldom the same twice in one work—were used in the *grand motet.* The German choir, from the days of Lutheran reforms, when choirs of men and women had begun to sing Psalms and Hymns in church and at home, had been the four-part component of natural voices, soprano-alto-tenor-bass; but the French choir maintained the late Renaissance five-part texture of soprano-alto-tenor-baritone-bass.

SUGGESTIONS FOR FURTHER STUDY

Records

Michel-Richard de Lalande: Te Deum. Musical Heritage Society MHS 514.
Mondonville: Cantate Domino. Music Guild, Westminster Records, MG-119.
The North German Baroque. Works by Praetorius, Decker, Weckmann, Bernhard, Kneller, Lubeck, Telemann. Haydn Society Records. HS-9043.
Purcell:Music for the Funeral of Queen Mary. Bach: Magnificat (BWV. 243). Seraphim, Angel Records, 60001.
A. *Scarlatti: Cantatas, "Il rossignolo" and "Clori Vezzosa e bella"* Oiseau-Lyre 50173.
Telemann, Buxtehude, Handel: Baroque Cantatas. Russell Oberlin, countertenor. Decca DL 9414.

Music

LALANDE, MICHEL-RICHARD DE. *De Profundis, Psaume CXXX Pour Soli, Choeurs, et Orchestre,* edited by Alexandre Cellier, London: United Music Publishers, c. 1944.
MONDONVILLE, JEAN-JOSEPH CASSANÉA DE. *Jubilate.* Transcribed and with introduction by Edith Borroff. University of Pittsburgh Press, 1961. (The instrumental parts are included.)
SHÜTZ, HEINRICH. *History of the Birth of Jesus Christ (1664)* New York: Bärenreiter (pocket score #132), 1966.

New Types of
Music
for Instruments

OVERTURE, RITORNELLO, AND INTERMEZZO

he violin and the soprano voice had much in common in the Baroque concept, both in their basic sound and in their function within the polar texture. Their differences were less important musically than their similarities; they were social differences which affected performance locations and audiences as well as the differences between sacred and secular texts in vocal music.

The combined consorts of the Renaissance band formed the basis of the instrumental contingents of early opera and oratorio, often with symbolic uses. Schütz, in the *Christmas Oratorio* (1664), for example, used a simple continuo for the recitativo (the common practice was to give the singer the greatest possible freedom), and for arias used strings with the angels, flutes and bassoon with the shepherds, trombones with the high priests, and trumpets with King Herod.

In early French opera the instrumental components were seldom specified on title pages, which called any mixed group a *symphonie*. Looking through a score whose overtures specify only "violins," one may find other movements marked "clarino" (trumpet specializing in high, active, often virtuoso music), or perhaps "flute tacit" (flute stop playing). It is necessary to go through an entire score to discover its instrumentation, and more instruments are often revealed to the scholar who examines the payrolls for given performances.

The opening of the Christmas Oratorio, for example, was titled *Introduktion oder Eingang* (Introduction or Entrance), and the instrumental introduction was marked *Sinfonia*—an Italian term for the instrumental group in general. But soon, the term meant a movement played by the group, and, in particular, the *overture*. In the Schütz, it was simply an extended phrase; in Lully it was a longer, three-section (slow-fast-slow) termed either *symphonie* or *overture*, while in Italy it would develop into an opposite three-section—fast-slow-fast—type, a difference reflecting the majestic entry of the King (or other VIP's) in the French productions and the desire to keep the public enlivened in the Italian.

The other interludes were most commonly dances (and in France, where they were the most numerous, most commonly minuets). The dance pieces used the Renaissance dance form of two sections, each with a different final, and each repeated (*A A B B*, written with repeats *A* :‖: *B* :‖). This two-section form was the single most important instrumental form of the Baroque era, as vital to the instrumental art as the *aria da capo* was to the vocal.

In their accompanying role, instruments also provided introductory and concluding strains for arias; these were labeled *sinfonia* by Schütz. However, because it provided a kind of refrain, especially when the aria proper began and ended with it, such a phrase was called a *ritornello*, the Italian for "refrain."

A middle movement was given the name "interlude," in Italian *intermezzo*, and although the term never really lost that meaning, it took on another meaning by the end of the Baroque, that of a short, light opera played between the acts of a longer, serious one.

SOLO SONATA

Instruments were also developing independent forms within the new style. The first and most natural was the piece for solo treble instrument and basso continuo, parallel to the solo cantata, and called the sonata. Such works were composed for a number of instruments, but in its general vogue, the violin would soon overtake the others; the next one hundred and fifty years would belong to the violin in a very special sense. It was the Baroque instrument of instruments, though the pipe organ was redefined in Baroque terms to the extent of having an equal claim for the German Baroque.

The first publication with the title *sonata*, for violin and basso continuo, was the first volume of *Affetti Musicali* (1617) by Biagio Marini (1597-1665) which also introduced the use of *opus* numbers. Expansion of the form was rapid; the string of contrasting movements remained the same, but two of Marini's sonatas, a decade apart, clearly demonstrate not only expansion but direction. The first, a seven-movement work 64 measures in toto, was marked "*Violino o cornetto*," for violin or cornett (the same as Gabrieli's); the second, also a seven-movement work, was 158 measures long, and was marked *Sonata per il violino per Sonar con due corde*, "Sonata for the violin to be played on two strings." It pointed to specific instrumental intention, since the playing on two strings at once (called double-stopping), producing two tones simultaneously, was obviously impossible on a cornett, flute, or other wind instrument. Thus the second work was for the violin, though that instrument was yet to attain its full popularity. (Antonio Stradivarius, perhaps the finest violin maker of all time, would not be born until about 1644; his incredible creative span reached from the 1660's almost to his death in 1736.) Marini's later sonata was also idiomatic and it pointed to the coming virtuoso difficulty. Double-stopping was common on the *viole da gamba*, which were tuned like lutes and were not infrequently used to realize figured basses, but was much more difficult on the newer violin and cello. Marini's sonatas of 1629 continued his experiments; they were marked "imaginative sonatas to be played in two and three parts on one violin, and other interesting modern innovations."

TRIO SONATA

The solo sonata continued through the century, but was supplanted in popularity by the sonata for two treble instruments and basso continuo, called a *trio sonata*. It had three written parts, but, with its two trebles and two-fold bass, it required four players, typically two violins, cello, and harpsichord. The trio sonata was to be, by gross weight, the most popular musical type of the Baroque era, partly because of its non-verbal versatility (which enabled it to be part of both church and court performances), and partly because it was less idiomatic and less difficult (which enabled it to become the music of the amateur musician), and finally because it required only four performers (which enabled it to fit into a modest room).

The first master of the trio sonata was Giovanni Legrenzi (1626-1690), an unusually versatile organist at Venice, the *Maestro da Capella* (Music Director) at St. Mark's Cathedral, which had a long tradition of instrumental as well as vocal music. Legrenzi wrote motets, Psalms, antiphonal (double-chorus) Masses, oratorios, and in addition he produced about twenty operas. But perhaps his finest contributions lay in the realm of instrumental music, notably the trio sonata to be performed in both the church (*chiesa*) and the court hall (*camera*), a social even more than a musical distinction.

The *sonata da chiesa* avoided dance titles (even when using dance types), using simple tempo designations. The two basic types were the *Adagio* (slow) and the *Allegro* (fast), representing the two basic moods or *Passions* and calling for different styles of performance. The *Adagio* was often a short movement of two or three phrases, all different, frequently—as the Adagio suggested—chromatic. It was often paired with an Allegro, for which purpose it might end on the dominant to prepare for the ensuing movement. The Allegro might be fugal, but it was more

Example 6

Third and fourth movements of the second sonata from *12 Sonate a tre, doi violini, e violone o arcileuto, col basso per l'organo* (Opus 3, 1689) by Corelli. The title incorporates the listing of four players for the three parts: in English it reads "12 Trio Sonatas, [for] two violins and bass viol or archlute, with a bass part for the organ."

The work is a representative sonata da chiesa, a four-movement Grave-Allegro-Adagio-Allegro format calling for organ in the basso continuo. The sonata is in *D* major, with three of the four movements in that tone. The third movement is in *b* minor, a modern and increasingly frequent contrast. The unprecedented popularity of Corelli's works is mirrored in the nineteen different editions of Opus 3 by 1715 (plus six others in collections of Opus 1-4).

The Adagio ends with a postscript, after the last arrival in *b* minor at Measure 38, a descent by step to the dominant, *F♯* major, in a progression rhythmically incorporating the hemiola proportion used as cadential ritard (see page 54). Harmonically, through use of the lower forms of the seventh and the sixth degrees of the scale, it presents a cadence called "Phrygian" because of the half-step between the sixth and fifth scale degrees (in this case *G* and *F♯*) characteristic of the old Phrygian mode (with final on *E*).

The juxtaposition of the *F♯* major final chord of the Adagio with the *D* major of the Allegro produces an effect of piquant harmonic color; it was common in the late Baroque. The two-section form of the Allegro, along with its fugal character and triple beat, is representative.

Not representative, but personal, is the turning of the subject upside down in the second half of the movement. Such *inversion* was more common as an episodic device in the formal fugue.

Example 6—*Continued*

Example 6—*Continued*

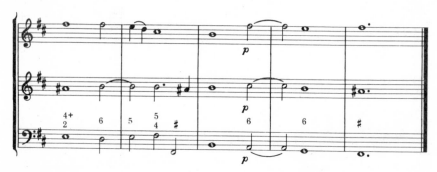

Example 6—*Continued*

Example 6– *Continued*

often a dance-like movement in the standard two-section form $(A:\|\!:B:\|)$. The *sonata da chiesa* generally had from three to six movements.

The *sonata da camera* was similar in principle, but it could freely name dance forms and profit from their popularity; in practice, the sonata da camera was like a suite of dances, probably preceded by an Adagio, and possibly containing one or two other non-dance movements. It tended to be longer than the *sonata da chiesa*.

By the beginning of the last quarter of the century, these types were well established and Italy was ready for the man who would provide their culmination and win an international reputation of incalculable influence, the Bolognese Arcangelo Corelli (1653-1713). As a violinist, Corelli was unequalled in his day, said to be both learned and full of feeling. His skill was legendary, advancing the technique of his modern instrument—now at its first peak—and yet when he played, it was said that it was usual for "his countenance to be distorted, his eyes to become red as fire, and his eyeballs to roll as in agony."[4]—an inspirational stance likely to give the castrati some healthy competition. Corelli is not known to have toured as a violinist, but he produced weekly concerts at the palace of Cardinal Ottoboni, and his Monday afternoons became essential experiences for the hundreds of young people who were sent on the "grand tour" of Europe to complete their education.

An English journalist of Corelli's time wrote of his impact on English music:

> . . . the numerous traine of yong travellers . . . that about this time went into Italy and resided at Rome and Venice, where they heard the best musick and learnt of the best masters. . . . Then came over Corellys first consort [trio sonata] that cleared the ground of all other sorts of musick whatsoever.[5]

It is doubtful that more than a handful of composers in the history of music have been so universally recognized as Corelli. His defining influence throughout Western music is all the more remarkable in view of the small number of his published works: one volume of solo violin sonatas, four volumes of trio sonatas, and one of *concerti grossi*. His trio sonatas were doubtless the most widely performed of his works, but the most innovative were the *concerti grossi*, of which form he was said to be the inventor.

---

[4]Sir John Hawkins, *A General History of the Science and Practice of Music* (1776), with a new introduction by Charles Cudworth. 2 vols. (New York: Dover Publications, Inc., 1963), II, 674.
[5]*Roger North on Music*. Transcribed from his essays of c. 1695-1728 and edited by John Wilson. (London: Novello and Company, Ltd., 1959), p. 310f.

CONCERTO GROSSO

The *concerto grosso* was in a sense the complement of the trio sonata. It was the large concert form, using a dozen or more players deployed in two groups, a small group of soloists (a trio sonata in Corelli's concerti grossi), and a larger group with three or four players on each part. It was a large concept needing a large hall, unsuited to amateur performance. It was truly modern, an exciting kind of experience for performers and listeners alike, a coming together of the many interests of the period: it was theatrical in its interplay of forces, it had elements of virtuosity, it centered in the voguish string instruments, and it made use of the full panoply of the new style.

The concerto grosso basically comprised an interaction of the two groups, the small group (*concertino*, a diminutive concerto) of soloists who balanced with dexterity and technical skill the large group (*concerto grosso*—the term had three meanings: the large group within the ensemble, the total ensemble of both groups, and a work performed by the total ensemble). The larger group used additional players who were called reinforcing or *ripieno* players; the larger group was always made of strings and continuo harpsichord, while the *concertino,* as the form developed, could include any instruments—woodwinds, strings, brasses, harpsichord, lute, mandolin—and, even when a solo harpsichord was included, had its own continuo harpsichord.

The central appeal of the concerto grosso resided in the alternations of amount and quality of sound provided by the two groups, the spatial deployments in performance, and the heightening through these of the basic elements of the new style. A German visitor to Corelli's concerts wrote of his delight with this "ingenious mixture":

> For by exactly observing this opposition or rivalry of the slow and the fast, the loud and the soft, the fullness of the great choir and the delicacy of the little trio, the ear is ravished by a singular astonishment, as is the eye by the opposition of light and shade.[6]

As the new type developed, the concerto turned to a three-movment (fast-slow-fast) standard format that was ideal for the increasingly virtuoso concertino parts, for it is human nature to want to begin and end a concert piece with a display of prowess.

The concerto allegro developed its own form, an incorporation of the principle of alternation: sections for the concerto grosso alternated with sections for the concertino; the first were marked *tutti* (all), the second marked *solo.* The first presented subjects that returned, and for that reason was called a *ritornello;* the second worked out the technical

---

[6]Oliver Strunk, (trans. and ed.), *Source Readings in Music History.* (New York: W. W. Norton & Company, Inc., 1950), p. 451.

possibilities of the solo instruments in fragmentary busywork, with repetition rare, and was called an *episode*. The form was called a *ritornello* form, and a concerto allegro typically had four or five ritornelli. A typical form might have an opening ritornello in the tonal center of the work; an episode; a second ritornello presenting the subjects of the first, but in a different tonal center; an episode; a third, less stable ritornello, possibly modulatory; an episode; and a restatement of the first ritornello ($R^1e^1R^2e^2R^3e^3R^1$).

By the end of the century, a trend toward smaller, more virtuoso concertino groups was producing many concertos for two players; the city of Bologna was known for its trumpet concertos, featuring the *clarino* trumpets which had narrow bores and special mouthpieces for playing the high ornate passages that made the trumpet a competitive instrument in the Baroque art. Double concertos for two violins were also becoming popular.

The trio sonata was the most multitudinous form of the Baroque; but the concerto grosso was the most modern. It would change in the early years of the eighteenth century and be the chief avenue toward the coming classical style.

SUGGESTIONS FOR FURTHER STUDY

Records
Corelli: 4 Church Trio Sonatas, Op. 1; 4 Chamber Trio Sonata, Op. 2. Vox M 1229.
Corelli: Concerto Grosso D Dur, Op. 6, No. 1; Concerto Grosso C Moll, Op. 6, No. 3. Apon Record Co., P.O. Box 131, Grand Central Station, New York, N.Y. HM 25140.
Henry Purcell: Trio Sonatas (from the second book of ten). Dover HCR-5224.

Books
HUTCHINGS, ARTHUR. *The Baroque Concerto.* London: Faber and Faber, 1961.

CHAPTER

6

The Baroque Ideal
Reaches Its Height

A WORLD EXPLORING

 he seventeenth century was perhaps the richest of modern times in its scope of exploration—not only geographically, but also physically, philosophically, and scientifically—and of reference to both old and new. It was the century of the microscope, but a time when witches were still being burned; it was the century of discovering the circulation of the blood, yet surgeons were still bleeding and leeching; it was the time when alchemists and astrologers were working at the side of chemists and astronomers. In short, it was a century very conscious of the new ideas percolating throughout the west, yet still more comfortable with the old vocabulary.

The seventeenth-century man was an adventurer (an arm-chair adventurer if nothing else) who delighted in diversity, who displayed continuing and omnivorous curiosity.

Music among both the arts and sciences has traditionally been regarded with respect from all sides; in the Baroque era, the expanding disciplines looked at music anew. It was an age of instruments, and the instruments of music were collected, exhibited, and measured; it was an age of mechanisms, and the human voice was examined as a mechanical phenomenon; it was an era of measurement, and the elements of music, including time, pitch intervals, and instruments, were subjected to the inventor's art and the observer's callipers. A *chronometer*, a huge metronome, was invented in France, where also the first technique was developed for the measurement of absolute frequency (1702)—interestingly, presented to the scientific Academy by a deaf acoustician, Joseph Sauveur (1653-1716), who also had theories on tempered tuning.

Acoustics, psychology (considered a branch of mechanics), statistics, and economics were all seventeenth-century sciences, and each interacted with music directly and indirectly. Exploration of the world was continuing, and the musical instruments of many cultures were the subject of study, for these could be measured as the music itself could not be. A collection of drawings of musical instruments, the *Gabinetto Armonico* (Musical Museum) by Filippo Bonanni, a Jesuit Museum curator, was published in 1716 and expanded in 1723. It was anthropological rather than acoustical in its approach, cataloguing serious, popular, folk, and exotic instruments—152 illustrations in all— pictured with their performers playing or holding them. These included nine African instruments, including the *sansa,* the xylophone, and the musical bow, and two instruments of the North American Indians—a gourd rattle from Virginia and a coiled bark trumpet from Florida.

MUSICAL EXCITEMENT: THE BEAT

Probably the chief excitement of the music of the seventeenth century was its beat and the perception of the beat as accumulating in regular groupings called meter.

It is hard to recapture the reactions of past audiences to their first realizations of what we now take for granted. In order to comprehend the excitement of beat and meter, it is necessary to understand the rhythmic system that had served Medieval and Renaissance music. It had been a *proportional system,* in which all parts had individually coordinated with a standard speed regulator called the *tactus* (in Italian the *batutta*), an up-and-down motion of the hand which remained at something like the speed of the human pulse. The tactus was like a metronome always at 72 to 84 beats per minute; a musician could use the metronome for pieces with widely varying speeds, without changing its setting, by proportioning his speed appropriately: one or two quarter-notes per tick, most simply, or, to achieve subtler tempos, three quarter-notes to two ticks, five to three, or vice versa. At the height of the proportional system, the means of accommodation were so numerous and the technique so complex that over three dozen proportion signs were in use, and two colors of ink were required in notation.

At the end of the sixteenth century, Morley, in his *Plaine and Easie Introduction to Practicall Musick* (1597) had still charted 45 rhythmic proportions, but in the dialogue between teacher and student (the standard manner of a Renaissance text book), the student responded to seeing the chart by saying that such a table is "more than I ever mean to beat my brains about," and the teacher reassured him that few of the proportions were still in use.[7] In fact, two remained, along with two of the proportion signs.

First, the definition of note values in the proportion of two to one (♪♪ = ♩, ♩♩ = 𝅗𝅥, etc.) remained, along with the dot to increase the length of a note. In the Baroque era, the exact length of a dotted note was still variable in many instances, however. And second, the proportion of two to three, called the *hemiola* (Greek for "one and a half") remained in its simplest usage of beats of—in modern terms— freely alternating quarter and dotted quarter, in metric terms freely alternating ¾ and ⅜. A popular rhythm in the early Baroque used a regular alternation of these values, using a meter sign 3:

The two proportion signs that remained in use were c and ¢; c was a broken circle indicating the simple proportion of one *breve* to the tactus, the breve to be divided into two groups of two, roughly, ⁴⁄₄ meter. (*Breve* literally meant a short note, which it had originally been, but by the end of the sixteenth century, it was a long note; it was notated like the modern whole-note, which is still called a *breve* in British usage.) ¢ porportioned the breve to the half-tactus rather than the tactus, resulting in tempo twice as fast, roughly comparable to ²⁄₂ or "cut time."

By the end of the Baroque, the hemiola proportion had become a cadential device comparable to a modern ritard. In triple meter, a hemiola was introduced to slow the music down (the hemiola is bracketed).

The cadential hemiola was a shift from ♩. to 𝅗𝅥 as a beat; in practical terms it introduced one measure of three half-notes instead of three quarter-notes. It was most often notated 𝅗𝅥 𝅗𝅥 𝅗𝅥 (without change of meter sign) or 𝅗𝅥 ¢ 𝅗𝅥 |; it was a true proportional shift, and not a syncopation.

The essential excitement of the new Baroque beat was that it completely reversed the practical procedure of the proportional system: instead of coordinating variously to a universal beat, the performer now coordinated in two or three simple ways to a beat that changed according to the speed of the piece, an effect that must have seemed absolutely astounding in the seventeenth century.

COMMON COIN

As various as were the Baroque forms—opera, cantata, oratorio, grand motet, solo sonata, trio sonata, concerto grosso—in their media and total effect, they shared ideals and basic techniques; these defined the Baroque style at its height.

---

[7]Thomas Morley, *A Plain and Easy Introduction to Practical Music,* edited by R. Alec Harman. (London: J. M. Dent and Sons Ltd., 1952), p. 58.

The most obvious observation would be that virtually all of the terms of the new style were Italian, an observation reflecting the Italian leadership of the Baroque style which was unquestioned and definitive; the vocabulary of music would be Italian for three hundred years. The terms not Italian (the grand motet form and the names for wood-wind instruments are French) tell us of the exceptional contributions of other nationalities.

Second, they all used the basso continuo, which was essential to the Baroque concept of fabric, sound, and structure. The polar fabric combined the melodic exteriors with harmonic middle register, and conceived of structure (harmonic and formal) as resident in the bass. The basso continuo was so taken for granted that even the title "sonata for violin alone" meant a sonata for one violin (rather than two) and basso continuo; it was assumed in performing groups, with the exception only of keyboard and lute solo pieces, a few persisting traditional types (such as English consort music for viols), and groups, where its use was impractical (such as the town bands of Germany, who performed from the tower of a city hall and in processions). It defined the Baroque sound in the broadest sense, and also defined Baroque theory and form in the finest sense.

Third, they shared a love of color, of tone quality. The Baroque era was one of diversity, and the musician rejoiced in the diversity of sound which his great number of instruments permitted him. Gamba and cello flourished side by side: a solo gamba sonata might well use a cello in its continuo, or vice versa. Recorder and flute flourished side by side as well, and one composer might use the two in the same work to enjoy their differences. Lute and guitar flourished, as well as an array of instruments soon to become obsolete in a new philosophy that would select a few instruments and discard the rest.

Fourth, they shared an informing love of contrast which virtually defined Baroque musical structure, and which was not only decorative, but actively impelling. The polar fabric incorporated simultaneous contrasts of color, line, and function; but contrasts in succession, contrasts by juxtaposition and alternation, were the essentials of the achievement of size—length or largeness of sound. The contrast between the free recitativo and the structured aria, the contrast between a solo aria and a choral movement, between familiar and learned styles, between vocal and instrumental movements, between adagio and allegro, between concerto grosso and concertino, ritornello and episode—all were aspects of the exploitation of contrast basic to the Baroque ideal. Musicians spoke of the *stile concertato*, the style of competing and accommodating elements, much as they did light and shadow in painting—Rembrandt was a Baroque painter. The contrasts of music included architectural placement in performance, which meant that the listener would enjoy

Plate V

An instrument maker's workshop. Illustration from the *Grande Encyclopédie* (1751) issued by the French group headed by Denis Diderot and Jean-Jacques Rousseau. Violins, violas, a guitar, and a lute are hanging overhead. On the wall in back are a cittern (long-necked guitar), a trumpet, and a bass cornett (appropriately called a serpent). Harps, bassoons, a chamber organ, and, leaning against the wall at right, a tromba marina take up the middle ground. A cello leans against the wall at the back, and a hurdy-gurdy is on the floor in the foreground.

Courtesy of The University of Michigan Library, Ann Arbor.

varying directions, music reaching him from the right and the left, from the front and the back. And the variety and alternation of forces carried with it a variety and alternation of dynamic value as well; the two groups of the concerto grosso, for example, by being large and small, were automatically loud and soft as well—contrasts written into the very fabric of the music and residing in it rather than in dynamic control by individual performers.

Baroque types shared the concept of performance as a mixture of clarity and mood, of technical skill and passion. The passions themselves incorporated a basic contrast between the adagio and the allegro types, with many others between creating a polar aspect of interpretation that defined the virtuoso.

And finally, they shared the basic theory of music.

BAROQUE THEORY

Basic to Baroque theory were the concepts of meter, tone, and subject.

Meter was a combining of beats, a steady, motivating pulse grouped into a regular pattern of *measures* by giving accents to every second, third, or fourth beat—called *metric accents*. The meter signature of the Baroque era told the performer about the tempo of the piece as well as the expectation of type of measure; dance titles were also indications of both meter and tempo. As the tempo became less clear, tempo indications bcame more common. Meter signatures could be subtle: $\mathbf{C}$, $\mathbf{2}$, $\frac{2}{4}$; 3, $\frac{3}{2}$, and $\frac{3}{4}$ all indicated different tempos. Later editors reduced the number of meter signs to conform with nineteenth-century practice, but modern editors are returning to original signatures.

Tone was a concept of key-center, replacing the modal concept of Medieval and Renaissance theory. A tone was a seven-note octave scale defined by its tonic, its dominant (a fifth above the tonic), and its mediant (a third above the tonic), named because of its position between tonic and dominant. The dominant was immutable: a perfect fifth above the tonic; but the mediant was mutable, an imperfect third above the tonic, to be either major or minor. Thus the tone was defined as having two elements: the location of its tonic note and the nature of its mediant. The tones numbered eight at the middle of the Baroque: *d, g, a, e, C, F, D*, and *G* (small letters indicating minor and capitals major).

A keyboard tuned c, c♯, D, E♭, E, F, F♯, G, G♯, A, B♭, and B♮ could negotiate these eight tones, but sixteenth-century theorists had gone much further, experimenting with keyboards tuned in quarter-steps and composing enharmonic madrigals, and the other tones were known and used, defined through transposition.

The tone incorporated an expectation of arrival, of ending, as the theorist Guillaume-Gabriel Nivers put it in his treatise of 1667, "on a chord which the ear appears to expect in a natural way," a pull toward the tonal center which defined the idea of *tonality* and which comprised an essential excitement and modernity of Baroque theory. Baroque audiences enjoyed tone for its own sake; modulation was defined by the theorist of 1667, but, he cautioned, it was "practiced only among the learned."

Tonality implied harmonic progression, and this was a function of the bass, "the foundation and the basis for all composition." The bass was often *static*, activating the tonic note through repetition or octave leaps, enabling the soloist(s) to explore the tone melodically at leisure; the bass could be *active,* leading through the tone or modulating to another tone; and the bass could be *cadencing,* leading to the satisfaction of conclusion upon the expected tonic chord, generally through a series of short cadential feints (deceptive resolutions, expecting the tonic but going elsewhere) and repetitive completions to the tonic (authentic resolution).

Subject worked out meter and tone through a characteristic melodic shape, conceived generally as a structural germ or motive. According to the theorist of 1667, it was "created by the force of the imagination," and it determined the character and the mood of the music. Study of composition centered in the relationship between subject and bass, which culminated in the culminating step of fugal technique, the "step of perfection." Interestingly, this was the bringing of the old learned or "worked" techniques into the new style. Fugue in Baroque theory was an imitative working-out of a subject, in a polyphonic fabric accommodated to the new ideal of tone and in a structure related to the ritornello principle in its alternation of subject sections and episodes.

All three basic elements were in a sense transitional, between Medieval-Renaissance and Classic-Romantic concepts. The Baroque beat was a phase between the proportional and fully metric concepts. The Baroque concept of tone was a half-way house between Medieval-Renaissance hexachord and mode and Classical-Romantic *key.* The eight original tones became *keys* by the end of the Baroque; *key* was still a tonal center, any center, with its dominant and subdominant, but with the character of the mediant a matter of color: G and g were two separate tones, but by 1750 were regarded as different colors—major and minor—of the single key of G. And subject, the latest concept to mature and the latest to be transformed, provided a transition, through the Classical era, to the Romantic idea of *theme.* Subject and theme existed together in Classical style and even into early Romanticism; the opening of the Beethoven Fifth Symphony (1807) was subject rather than theme.

EMBELLISHMENT

A vital element in Baroque music was contained in the many forms of enlivening the basic structure, chiefly through additions called *embellishments* or *graces.* In order to maintain a clear picture of the essentials, embellishments were frequently abbreviated in special signs, which could be interpreted with a certain freedom and taste. But a soloist was expected also to "improve" his part, that is to turn it to good account, fulfill it, to complete it with added notes, preferably spontaneously. The relation between "improve" and "improvise" is an interesting one.

Baroque music is misleading in its written form because the harmonic frame, largely consonant, was notated, while the embellishments, which introduced the complementary dissonances, were abbreviated or not written down at all. Yet dissonance was considered a necessary balance, the salt of music, which did not smother consonance, according to a definition of harmony published in 1703, but served "on the contrary to make them all the more sensitive and brilliant, through the happy and wise opposition of these two contraries."[8]

Dissonances were passing or accented. The passing were fleeting, slurred, and often extended, either in a parabolic fioratura or in a *tirata* or "rip," connecting two essential tones. More important were the accented embellishments, particularly the *appoggiatura* or "leaning" tone, which was a heavily stressed displacement of a consonant tone, to which it eventually resolved in a slurred progression. An English journalist described them shortly after 1700:

> Those notes should be prest hard; for the elegance and surprise excites a great attention, as if the auditors were upon tip-to to know what would become of this business.[9]

The trill was an important embellishment, conceived as a series of falling *appoggiature,* beginning on the upper note (even when that must be repeated), and, like the appoggiatura, taking on the mood of the piece, slow in a slow movement and quick in an allegro.

The improvising of variation, the "improving" of repeated strains with diminutions, divisions, and embellishments, was a cherished skill of the Baroque. It culminated in a technique of improvised variations over a repeated bass phrase called a *basso ostinato,* or *ground,* which implied a melodic and harmonic pattern. In England, a vogue for improvising upon a ground led to continued interest in the viol (viola da gamba), whose fleetness gave it an advantage in such music.

In France, viol players "improvised upon a subject"; a viol method text said it was difficult.

> This kind of Playing demands more science, more spirit, and more technique than all the others: it consists in five or six notes given to a man on the spot, & on this few notes, as on a canvas, the man works to fill his Subject a few times with harmony in an infinity of ways, & proceeding from diminution to diminution; so that he makes us find as many tender Airs, and a thousand other diversities, as his inspiration can furnish to him.[10]

---

[8]Sébastien de Brossard, *Dictionnaire de Musique,* (1703), facsimile edition. (Amsterdam: Antiqua, 1964).
[9]Roger North, (ed. Wilson), *op. cit.,* p. 219.
[10]Jean Rousseau, *op. cit.,* p. 71.

Plate VI

A. Embellishment in a Corelli slow movement. Facsimile from an English edition of the solo sonatas (Opus 5), about 1730. (The same as in Example 13.) The bottom staff is the basso continuo, the middle staff is the solo part of the *Grave* as notated in the original edition (1700), and the top staff gives proposed divisions.

Plate VI—*Continued*

Courtesy of Library of Congress, Washington, D. C.

Plate VI—*Continued*

Trill. On a shorter note, the trill would be shorter, generally of four notes.

Trill with appoggiatura.

Trill with turn.

Turn.

Mordent. On a shorter note, the mordent would be shorter, generally of three notes.

Appoggiature.

Appoggiatura and mordent combined.

Staccato.

Aspiration.

Arpeggiations, simple and figured. The direction of the slash indicated the direction of the arpeggiation.

SUGGESTIONS FOR FURTHER STUDY

Records

The *400th Anniversary: Claudio Monteverdi, Scherzi Musicali*, Project, PR 7001 SD contains hemiola changes: "Damigella tutta bella" is an example.

The Baroque beat has been the subject of delight in the popular field, with such issues as *Bach's Greatest Hits*, a scat style of transcription by the Swingle Singers (Philips, PHS 600-097), Jazz Guitar Bach (Nonesuch, H-71069), and the Baroque Beatles Book (Elektra, EKL-306).

Books and Music

ARNOLD, F. T. *The Art of Accompaniment from a Thorough-Bass as Practiced in the 17th and 18th Centuries.* London: The Holland Press, 1961.

COHEN, ALBERT (Trans.) *Guillaume Gabriel Nivers: Treatise on the Composition of Music* (1667). Brooklyn 23, N.Y.: Institute of Medieval Music (1653 W. 8th St.), 1961.

DONINGTON, ROBERT. *The Interpretation of Early Music.* London: Faber and Faber, c. 1963. Many quotes delightfully arranged and connected.

KOCH, CASPAR. *The Organ Student's Gradus ad Parnassum.* New York: J. Fischer and Bros., c. 1945. In paperback (1969) as *The Piano Student's Gradus ad Parmassum.* An excellent survey of Baroque and Classical embellishments arranged in practical and easily available form.

MORLEY, THOMAS, edited by R. Alec Harman. *A Plain and Easy Introduction to Practical Music.* London: J. M. Dent and Sons, Ltd., 1952.

Several of the Swingle Singers arrangements have been issued in Octavo by B. F. Wood Music Co., Inc. The Bach *Fugue in D. Major* (#44-851) is good to begin such studies with; singing his two and three part *Inventions* —or any other instrumental work—is valuable.

B. Table of *agréments*. Facsimile from the *Pièces de Clavessin* (1724), by Jean-Philippe Rameau. The column on the left gives the name of the ornament with its abbreviated form of notation; the column on the right gives its realization.

The realization of the *coulez* attempted to notate the legato of the resolution. Legato itself, like vibrato, was considered an ornamental technique.

Of these signs, only the suspension (keyboard aspiration) was at odds with other composers' use of the symbol. In his innovative combining of the keyboard piece with the solo aria in the *Pièces de clavecin avec voix ou violon* (1748), Jean-Joseph Cassanéa de Mondonville used the Rameau symbol above a trill sign to indicate a trill with appoggiatura.

Continuing
the
Older Traditions

LUTE AND GUITAR MUSIC

he art of the lute was maintained without interruption through the Baroque era. The lute dance of the Renaissance was the basis of the suite of lute dances, preceded by an improvised movement, or a movement composed in an improvisatory style, called a *prélude* (in French, *préluder* meant "to improvise"); this was often notated without rhythm, so that the performer could create his own. The other movements in the suite would all be dances, all metered and in the two-section dance form.

In Spain, the guitar replaced the lute, and in France the two flourished together. Louis XIII had studied violin as a toddler and the harpsichord and lute later; the guitar was the instrument of Louis XIV, who had a daily guitar lesson even in late middle age.

The bass lutes, notably the *theorbo* and the *chittarone*, were used as alternatives to the harpsichord in the realization of figured bass; all kinds of lutes were used to accompany songs.

In Germany many of the small courts maintained lutenists in lieu of a larger contingent; many of them were trained in France after the middle of the century, when the center of the lutenist's art moved northward from Italy. Sets of hymns and sacred songs for voice and lute were published in Germany.

In Italy, lute, cittern, mandora, and its small cousin, the mandolin, were widely used. The lute and mandolin appeared occasionally in the concertino of the concerto grosso.

Plate VII

A. Lute instruments. Plate XVI of the second volume of *Syntagma Musicum* (1618) by Michael Praetorius.

1 and 2 are bass lutes (theorbo or chitarrhone); 3 is a standard lute; 4 is a guitar; 5 is a small mandolin called the *mandolino milanese* or *pandurina*; 6 is a gittern, a form of a guitar; 7 is a smaller gittern; 8 is a pocket fiddle or *kit*.

Courtesy of The University of Michigan Library. Ann Arbor.

Plate VII—*Continued*

B. Gentleman playing a theorbo. Late seventeenth-century engraving. The long neck and unfingered strings, which bypass the fingerboard directly to the second group of pegs, are clearly shown.

Courtesy of the Stellfeld Purchase, The University of Michigan Library, Ann Arbor. Photo by R. E. Kalmbach.

Example 7

Suite in g minor for theorbo, from *Deliciæ testudinis* (Delicacies for the Lute), 1667, by Esaias Reussner (1636-1679).

This suite has no prelude, but is a set of dances and airs, all in the two-section a :||: b :|| form that was the staple of the Baroque suite. The order of the movements—Allemanda, Courant, Sarabanda, Aira, Gigue, Aria—is representative of the generally flexible suite. By the end of the century most suites (and many sonatas) would end with a gigue.

The chief embellishments are the appoggiatura, the short trill (+), and the arpeggiation, either upward (/) or downward (\). The mordent is used in the Courant. In addition, the acciaccatura (literally, a crushing) appears, written out as a second, at Measure 5 and at the final cadence of the Allemanda. Appoggiature are represented as small added notes; their time value was free, but in general they were savored and prolonged.

The suite evinces both French and Italian influences. Reussner was trained by his father and also by a virtuoso of the French tradition. A Silesian by birth, he was a court lutenist in both Breslau and Berlin at courts emulating French manners. He supervised entertainments and doubtless provided basso continuo realizations as well; he notated his lute music in French tablature.

The lowest note of the fingered range was A, (the tuning, in contrast to the British custom, was f^1, d^1, a, f, d, A). The five added strings were tuned variably, in this case G, F, E♭, D, and CC; these five were the longer strings to the side of the fingerboard (and thus, once tuned, not changeable), the presence of which distinguished the theorbo from the lute.

For study purposes, this edition represents the notation on two staves and at the actual pitches; modern lute and guitar editions generally use only the treble clef, transposing the music up an octave. For the lute and guitar ranges, the single clef is satisfactory, but the added five notes of the theorbo extend the range so far below that the single staff is inadequate. The tablature was so suited to the needs of the music that many lutenists today are learning to use the early editions.

Example 7— *Continued*

Example 7–*Continued*

Example 7—*Continued*

Aria

Gigue

Example 7—*Continued*

WIND MUSIC

The brass consort, Renaissance *high music,* had been continued in Germany, where civic affairs required town bands, called trumpeters or pipers. The new style was not practical for these groups, for they played while marching, or from the tower (*Türm*) of the town hall; a literature of *Türmsonaten,* polyphonic works in the consort tradition, reached its apex in the last third of the seventeenth century. Johann Christoph Pezel (1639-1694), a violinist, trumpeter, and composer in Leipzig, left over four dozen such works, including *Intraden à 4* (Processional Pieces for Four Players, 1683), and *Fünff stimmigte blasende Musik* (Five-voiced Wind Music, 1685).

In addition, a great deal of brass music was written for fanfares and for hunting and coach signals, all of it in a continuation of the old style. Hunting calls were often short-two-section forms for one or two horns, trumpets, or both. The hunting and coach signals were common sounds, known to everyone, and the trumpet tune was a popular type during the late Baroque, used as subjects in works for all instruments.

Trumpets, oboes, and drums were the instruments of mounted forces, playing consort music in the higher registers. Particularly in France, this music was given serious attention and contributed to the technique of these instruments as they were being incorporated into the opera orchestra—often the location of innovation in the history of instrumentation. At the beginning of operatic performance, the instrumentalists comprised a group of combined consorts, plus lutenists and players of the small organ, called *positif,* because it could be moved by three or four men and put into place as desired. In France, Lully used the string group, *Les 24,* a ripieno string group, as a basic cadre, adding other instruments for color, as added consorts; a dance might be played by oboes and bassoon, or might add these to the strings. The modern concept of orchestra would await the end of the Baroque and point the way toward the Classical style.

VOCAL MUSIC

Like other types of music that continued in the old forms, vocal music did so whenever it was inconvenient to use a basso continuo or where a special pleasure of the music lay in its style. Three main types were maintained through the Baroque era.

First was the polyphonic church composition, most frequently a motet or, in Germany, a simple chorale, set for voices alone. The motet for double choir was at its apex in the early years of the Baroque, and it persisted in decreasing numbers through the seventeenth century and

Plate VIII

Hunting call used by hunters at the French court in the third quarter of the seventeenth century, attributed to Louis XIV.

Courtesy of the Stellfeld Purchase, The University of Michigan Library, Ann Arbor.

The text reads: "THE ROYAL LOUIS. Fanfare made by the King himself at Fontainbleau: it was sounded at the sighting of a stag with magnificent antlers"——one with his fourth head, i.e., in the fourth year of his antlers. (All French musical descriptive titles are given feminine endings.)

The bottom line G clef, known as the French violin clef, is used in this engraving from a general text of 1734, in a supplement called *Tons de Chasse et Fanfares a Une et Deux Trompes*, "Hunting Calls and Fanfares for One and Two Horns." All of the calls in the 32-page supplement are in *D*. The calls are simple bugle tunes; the fanfares are in the two-section form characteristic of dance tunes, or, as in this case, in a *da capo* form with the first section to be repeated— in full, *a a b a.*

Example 8

Two seventeenth-century vocal canons.

A. A convivial round by Henry Purcell.

A 3 Voices

When V and I to - ge - ther meet, we

Yet I and V may meet once More, and

But when that V from I am gone, a -

make up VI in House or Street

then we two can make but IV

las poor I can make but I

B. A German devotional canon by Christoph Bernhard (1628-1692).

T   B

Herr, so du willst Un - recht zu - mes - sen,

wer wird be - stehn, wer wird be - stehn vor dei - nem

An -   ge - sicht.

Example 8—*Continued*

The Purcell represents the riddle canon, a gentler humor than the obstreperous catch. Its text is a pun on Roman numerals and the pronouns "you" and "I," made possible by the use of the Roman letter *V* to represent the letter *U*. The ditty thus begins, "When you and I together meet, we make up six in House or Street."

The use of B♭ in the signature, totally unnecessary and not characteristic of Purcell's generation (he died in 1695), reflects the practice of the second half of the eighteenth century: the round is taken from *The Catch Club, or Merry Companions,* published in 1762. Most of its 200 items (in two volumes) are in three parts, with about 30 in four.

The Bernhard is a two-part canon for tenor and bass, indicating its two voice ranges by use of different clefs, each part reading the same staff degrees in its own clef: fourth-line *C* (tenor) and fourth-line *F* (bass). Points of entry are indicated with initials. The solution reads:

into the eighteenth. Some of these works were published with continuo parts, but these were added, were not motivating, and provided a nod toward accepted modern practice without embracing its essence.

Second was the home and convivial song, generally sung without planned accompaniment and most often for voices without instruments; these flourished in the German devotional and drinking song and the English round, catch, and glee. Both of these types were for men's voices, and related to barbershop music—mentioned in Spain and England in the sixteenth century. The beer song was a folk or folk-like song, often harmonized by the singers on the spot, in simple two-parts or perhaps in basic chords in familiar style. Publications of songs were added in the eighteenth century, tending toward more formal song, with instruments.

Even popular songs were published with basso continuo; the popular songs in English included *The Vicar of Bray*, early versions of *Yankee Doodle*, and *The Girl I Left Behind Me*.

The English round or *catch*, on the other hand, has remained a Renaissance form to this day. The catch was a round canon constructed in such a way that the words took on new meaning as the canonic overlapping caused them to interact. The "catching" of the words into puns and new meanings, often bawdy, was a vein of humor made possible by the rich multiple heritage of the English language combining with the Renaissance canonic technique. It was impossible to "modernize" anything in a catch but the text and the chords as created by the overlapping voices. The British gentleman would not have wanted to modernize it; on the contrary, the founding of *Catch Clubs* in the seventeenth centuries assured that the jovial fellowship of catch singing would continue. Some catch clubs still meet.

The *glee*, from the old English term for minstrelsy, was a simple part-song in familiar style, to be sung by a group of men. The glee was an eighteenth- and nineteenth-century form, but it began in the Baroque, and the first of the *Glee Clubs* were Baroque socialities.

The third type of traditional vocal music was folk song, which has thrived in the West from the Medieval era, in some cases with little change. Dancing to songs accompanied with clapping, or played on a folk instrument, made folk song extremely versatile. The most popular folk instrument of the Baroque was the bagpipe—perhaps the universal folk instrument of the West. The seventeenth century contributed such refined versions as the French *musette* and Italian *sourdeline*, really harmonic instruments. The sourdeline had two chanters and two "drones," all keyed and capable of joining in the creation of harmony. The musette enjoyed considerable popularity in French society in the eighteenth century, as part of a general vogue for pastoral amusements.

In addition to these instruments of the people, Bonanni's *Gabinetto Armonico* also depicted the *zither* and *dulcimer* of the Eastern Europeans, the *kazoo* (called the *eunuch flute*) and the *comb-and-paper,* a variety of guitar types, drums, the Jew's (or jaw's) harp, and a few examples of the endlessly inventive percussion instruments, from bones to gourd rattles, that people have used to emphasize dance rhythms since time beyond knowing. Clapping, slapping, and stomping are probably universal percussion practices; they may lack sophistication and decorative potential, but make up for it in convenience and availability.

It was during the Baroque era that the violin was adopted as a dance instrument of the people. The Hardanger fiddle of Norway was famous, and the British fiddle made its way to the New World, where it furnished the tune for countless reels and barn dances, maintaining a Baroque technique that still flourishes today in country music.

SUGGESTIONS FOR FURTHER STUDY

Records

Catch as Catch Can. Experiences Anonymes, EA-0312.

French Lute Music, works by Charles Mouton, Robert de Visée, Pierre Attaignant, Jacques Bittner, and Le Sage de Richée. Musica Intima by Vox, TV 34137S.

The Glorious Sound of Brass. Includes a Türmsonate by Pezel. Columbia MS 6941.

Books and Music

BARBOUR, J. MURRAY. *Trumpets, Horns, and Music.* Lansing, Michigan: Michigan State University Press, 1964.

The Catch Club, or Merry Companions. First published by I. Walsh, London, 1762. Republished in facsimile (1965) by The Gregg Press, Inc., 171 E. Ridgewood Avenue, Ridgewood, New Jersey.

Der Kanon: Ein Singbuch für Alle, 1. Teil, Von den Anfangen bis Bach, edited by Fritz Jode, Wolfenbuttel, Germany: Moseler, n.d. An anthology of canons.

CHAPTER

~⊙⑩⊙~ 8 ~⊙⑩⊙~

Music in America

INDIANS AND SETTLERS

I n the New World, Spanish, French, and British colonies were expanding their domination over more and
more of the land.

The Indians, who were being pushed farther and
farther from their hunting grounds, were of several hundreds of tribes, each with a substantial culture and a lively
musical art. Essential to all of these cultures, as dissimilar as they
were from one another, was a view of music as a vital symbol of
life and of life functions. The music of Europe had become separated
from life, superimposed as a formal amusement upon an increasingly
specialized social structure, while for the professional musician it
was a total life pattern. For the Indian, it was more than either—it
was part of the total harmony of man and his world, a symbolic and
necessary accompaniment of all significant action from birth to death.

Indian music was both vocal and instrumental, basically polyphonic,
not in the restricted European sense of separately notated vocal lines,
but in the universal sense of simultaneous musical layers of sound,
melodic or percussive, independent yet related, often in highly sophisti-
cated ways. Indian rhythms were sometimes so intellectually complex
that to Europeans trained in simple proportions and meters they seemed
random, while melodic materials were kept simple, though subject to
variations in pitch that were not available in the European system.

In the seventeenth century, writings tended toward objective, even
appreciative accounts of Indian culture, but they were written by adven-

turers or scientifically minded explorers trained in almost anything but music. It is known that in the seventeenth century, whites attended Indian celebrations (in New England, the Indian Thanksgiving ceremonies and clambakes were attended by whites). The Algonquin dance contest, called the *cantico,* was popular as well; one colonial noted that "many a time Indians and settlers cut a cantico together."[11] The Indians in turn were often guests at barn dances and hoedowns.

For their part, the settlers brought with them the informal music of their homelands. In the area to be the United States, these were mainly British in the east and Spanish in the southwest. Folk music was probably the one constant type, and many of the old folk melodies were international. The English folk song had a long tradition of wandering songs which were particularly suited to the pioneer, and songs of loneliness and the open spaces developed on the English models. Settlers staked out homesteads and other settlers convened to help get a house up. After erecting the roof-tree, the settlers' dancing began—and "raising the roof" entered the language as a rousing party. The fiddler, guitar player, or even the Jew's harper played for the *quadrilles* (square dances), and singers sang ballads during quiet interludes.

SALON

The towns had various musical offerings. The larger towns had "musical evenings" in private homes, and a few began concerts from about 1730. Baltimore, New Orleans, New York, Boston, Charleston, and Philadelphia were the predominant musical towns. In 1731, "a Concert of Music on Sundry Instruments" was given in Boston, and in 1732 a series of concerts followed by "Country Dances for the Diversion of the Ladies" were advertized in Charleston. A few early opera productions—such as Coffey's *The Devil To Pay* in Charleston in 1736 —were gaining momentum, but political concerns were paramount at the end of the Baroque, and musical events were on the decline, not on the rise. In the late 1750's, popular political songs were the most prominent music in the colonies.

The basis of formal music in most towns was the salon musicale and dance. The colonials kept up with the continental fads, and music was among the imports most eagerly awaited. Guitars, spinets, violins, flutes, and a great deal of music arrived regularly, and the salon musicale was a sign of gentility and position. The less wealthy had parlors rather than salons, but a small harpsichord, a flute, violin, or cello, and any of the numerous amateur singers sufficed for a musicale.

---

[11]Alvin M. Josephy, Jr. and the Editors of *American Heritage Magazine, The American Heritage Book of Indians.* (New York: 1961), p. 173.

SACRED MUSIC

In the seventeenth century members of many church groups came to the New World. The Spaniards, French, and the settlers of Maryland were Roman Catholics, and even in the sixteenth century the plainsong Mass was established in Mexico City where a choir school was founded by the Spanish within twenty years of its capture. Spanish missions dotted the southwest, but their music was simple, even spare. New Orleans and Baltimore managed more elaborate music.

The Anglicans, or English Episcopalians, brought their liturgy and their old country practice of hymns, anthems, and English Masses. New York was the center of English high and low church practice in the eighteenth century. A few small pipe organs were installed in churches; in 1753 the organist of the Cathedral of Bristol was brought to New York; he founded a choral society on the English model and produced the first performance of Handel's *Messiah* in America—in New York in 1770.

Many smaller, newly-formed denominations came to the shores of the New World to seek freedom of worship; their music was often interesting, but almost always a copy of European church music. The German Seventh Day Dunkers, for example, settled in Pennsylvania in the 1720's, where they founded the Ephrata community. Their services made use of the chorale, and in 1730 their *Ephrata Hymn Collection* was published by the young printer, Benjamin Franklin (1706-1790).

The earlier English arrivals who had settled in New England from 1620 had turned from the Church of England to establish their own more severe practices. They brought with them a literature of late Renaissance Psalms and hymns, which they passed to their successors largely by rote.

By the early years of the eighteenth century New England hymnody was in a state of confusion. The last years of the Baroque era saw various attempts to clarify and unify the literature of the hymns. About 1720 *A very plain and easy introduction to the whole Art of Singing Psalm Tunes*, by John Tufts, was published.

It would take a generation to bring the diverse practices to a working general *modus operandi*, and then the war with the French and, finally, the Revolutionary war, would delay the creation of American hymnody still further. But gradually a system of teaching and composing was formed, independent of current European techniques, though influenced by current music (as distinct from techniques) in the subconscious ways that crept in simply through its being heard.

In order to train parishioners to sing hymns correctly, singing schools were organized. Church musicians in the cities could train local choirs, but most villages were too small to support a resident musician. Typi-

Example 9

American tunes of the eighteenth century.

    A. *100 Psalm [Tune]*. One of the older tunes in the repertoire of Protestant hymnody. Facsimile from Robert Bremner's *The Rudiments of Music*, Second Edition, Edinburgh, 1764. Bremner's book is typical of those brought by British protestants to the colonies. The four parts are labeled Tr[eble], Con[tra], Ten[or] or Ch[ief] part, and Bass. The tune is in *G* major, with the signature sharp at both registers in the treble clefs.

Example 9— *Continued*

B. *C.* [Hundred] *Psalm Tune.* Facsimile from Josiah Flagg's *A Collection of the best Psalm Tunes in 2, 3 and 4 parts,* Boston, 1764. This book, one of the earliest to appear in the Colonies, was engraved by Paul Revere. Like most American song books, it places this tune in the key of A. Of the several features of Flagg's book, perhaps the most interesting is the use of the trill sign—another Baroque feature in a continuing tradition.

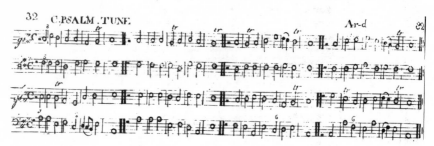

The Wing Collection, The Newberry Library, Chicago. With permission.

C. *Old Hundred.* The text of the hundredth Psalm was set to a new tune, and the old tune was given new words, with the title *Old Hundred* as a reminder of its prior association with the hundredth Psalm. Facsimile from *The Middlesex Collection of Church Music,* Second Edition, Boston, 1808. The tune is still in the tenor, but has been reharmonized and marked "L. M." L. M. is Long Meter, a verse form of four lines with eight syllables each (8.8.8.8.). It was second in popularity to the Common Meter, C. M. (8.6.8.6.—the same as the venerable "ballad meter"). Tunes were labeled for ease in substitution of hymn or tune; any verse in Long Meter could be sung to any tune labeled L.M.

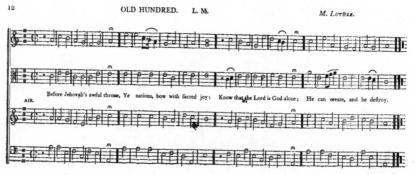

Courtesy of The University of Michigan Library, Ann Arbor. Photo by R. E. Kalmbach.

Example 9—*Continued*

D. *Chester*, by William Billings. Facsimile from Billings's *The New England Psalm Singer*, Boston, 1770. This book was engraved by Paul Revere.

The Clements Library, The University of Michigan, Ann Arbor. With permission.

cally the singing school was from six to twelve weeks long, created by subscription and taught by a journeyman musician, who boarded with some local citizen as did the regular school teachers. They taught note-reading on a Renaissance-derived *sol-fa* system, and they began to use hymn tunes by American-born composers. The new tunes were based on Renaissance theory, polyphonically conceived, in the familiar style, with the tune in the tenor.

The real start of the mature American singing school tradition dates from 1761, when the first book of tunes was published, but, more certainly, in 1770, with the publication of the *New England Psalm Singer* by William Billings (1746-1800), considered the finest of the composers of the coming "New England school." Billings was a "singular man," with a "magnificent voice," a friend wrote, "short of one leg, with one eye,"[12] a circumstance that kept him out of the war and at his post at a church in Boston, and may have been an important circumstance in founding the style.

By 1770, New England church singing had reached a state of excellence. The young patriot, John Adams, (to be the first vice president and second president of the United States), wrote in his diary of a village church he visited in 1771:

> Went to meeting in the afternoon and heard the finest singing that ever I heard in my life; the front and side galleries were crowded with rows of lads and lasses, who performed all their parts in the utmost perfection. I thought I was rapt up; a row of women all standing up and playing their parts with perfect skill and judgement, added a sweetness and springhtliness which absolutely charmed me.[13]

---

[12]Quoted in Alan C. Buechner's extended notes with *New England Harmony*, Folkways Records, FA 23771.
[13]Ibid.

The choir may have sung tunes from Billings' book, which included his most famous tunes, the round *When Jesus Wept* and the rousing *Chester*. The first was unique, the only round known from the tradition; the second was representative of the ideal of the movement, and was to become one of the most popular hymns of the Americans and a rallying tune of the Revolutionary War.

Plate IX

Frontispiece from William Billings' *New England Psalm Singer*, Boston, 1770. An engraving by Paul Revere.

The picture is a charming representation of the kind of vocal performance popular in England from the beginning of the seventeenth century.

The Clements Library, The University of Michigan, Ann Arbor. With permission. Photo by R. E. Kalmbach.

SUGGESTIONS FOR FURTHER STUDY

Records

The American Harmony, a Collection of Fugues and Plain Tunes (1779-1813). Washington Records, 1340 Connecticut Avenue, N.W., Washington, D. C. WR-418.

The New England Harmony, A Collection of Early American Choral Music. Folkways Recordings FA 2377. Good pamphlet of notes.

Schuman: New England Triptych. Columbia ML 5347. A 20th-century work on tunes by Billings; the second movement is based on *When Jesus Wept* and the last movement is based on *Chester.*

Books and Music

CHASE, GILBERT. *America's Music.* New York: McGraw-Hill Book Co., 1955.

EDWARDS, ARTHUR C. and MARROCCO, W. THOMAS. *Music in the United States.* Dubuque, Iowa: Wm. C. Brown Company Publishers, 1968.

HAVIGHURST, WALTER, editor. *Land of the Long Horizons,* (American Vista Series: The Midwest). New York: Coward-McCann, Inc., c. 1960.

JOSEPHY, ALVIN M., JR. and the Editors of *American Heritage Magazine. The American Heritage Book of Indians.* New York: American Heritage Publishing Co. Inc., 1961.

MARROCCO, W. THOMAS and GLEASON, HAROLD. *Music in America: An Anthology from the Landing of the Pilgrims to the Close of the Civil War, 1620-1865.* New York: W. W. Norton & Co., Inc., 1964.

McLANATHAN, RICHARD. *The American Tradition in the Arts.* New York: Harcourt, Brace & World, Inc., 1968. Excellent picture of colonial life as a whole.

Keyboard Music

RENAISSANCE TYPES

t the end of the Renaissance, instrumental music was established as valid; by the end of the Baroque era, it was established as vital. Yet even throughout the eighteenth century, estheticians could still be heard who felt that without words, music must founder in aimlessness and was by definition "trifling." To these men, meaning in music had to be directed by words. "To know what all this fracas of sonatas would mean, with which we are loaded," wrote the encyclopedist Jean-Jacques Rousseau in his *Dictionary of Music* (1768), "we must do as the ignorant painter, who was obliged to write under his figure, 'This is a tree.' 'This is a man.' 'And this is a horse.'" Yet even Rousseau had to admit that in his day the instrumental art was supreme. "Now," he wrote, "instruments form the most important part of music."

The instrumental types and structures that developed in the seventeenth century and the first half of the eighteenth century were of two main types: those which combined instruments and used the basso continuo, and those which, for reasons of practicality, could not. Musically, these can also be classified in general as modern and conservative in structural principle, for the polar ideal of monody, which was the *stile moderno*, required the basso continuo, and those types omitting it had to rely on Renaissance principles to create their music, while modernizing its harmonic-tonal structure, its rhythmic basis, and its subjects or melodic motives, but not its structural principles.

In the early seventeenth century. the basic keyboard instruments were the organ and clavichord (in Italy and the Low Countries) and the virginals (in the British Isles). The organ had been both a church and home instrument as long as it had remained a *positif*—small enough to be moved. But in the seventeenth century the organ became an architectural instrument, part of the church edifice, a physically huge body of pipes that could not be used in most palaces, much less in a modest salon.

Plate X

Mechanism of a pipe organ. Engraving from *l'Art du facteur d'orgues* (The Art of Organ Building, 1766-1778) by Dom François Bedos de Celles.

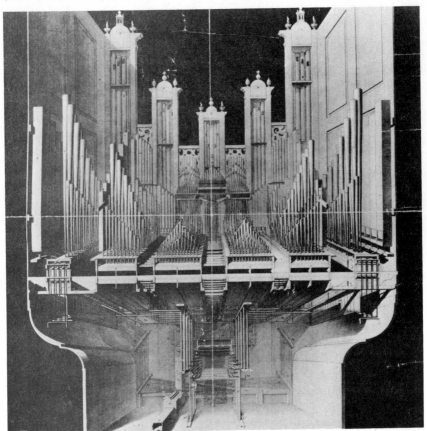

Courtesy of the Stellfeld Purchase, The University of Michigan Library, Ann Arbor.

This huge three-volume work, a summary of Baroque construction, was illustrated by fold-out engravings of extraordinary proportion and detail.

The larger portion of the illustration shows the architectural instrument, the ranks of pipes organized in space. The lower portion shows the mechanical instrument, the control and connecting devices. The scale of size can be appreciated by locating the console, of three manuals and a pedal keyboard, at the bottom.

It became a special instrument, associated with the church, and, as might be expected, it achieved special greatness in the German states, where the churches were central to musical practice.

As "keyboard instruments," the smaller salon types were—and are— more often designated, though many publications through the last quarter of the seventeenth century still projected themselves to a general market of any instrument with a keyboard. Only when enough homes had instruments and enough organs had pedal boards did publications separate the two categories, and an increasing difference between church and home types of music caused the separation quickly to become complete and to remain distinct, once it was made.

The Renaissance types—toccata, fantasy, and ricercar, among others —used a basic punctus form which expanded into sectional form. A phrase of one texture would be followed by another phrase in a contrasting texture. The imitative point alternated with the phrase in the familiar style, and as the Baroque concept of rhythm became firmly established, slower phrases alternated with faster phrases. All of them expanded gradually to sections rather than phrases; double bars between sections were introduced, and the size expanded.

THE GERMAN ORGAN SCHOOL

The important organists in the early years of the seventeenth century were those of the Low Countries and Italy, represented by Jan Pieterszoon Sweelinck (1562-1621) and Girolamo Frescobaldi (1583-1643). These men carried the Renaissance forms into expanded size. Their German students carried them further and established the German organ school as one of the consummate Baroque types. Samuel Scheidt (1587-1654) studied with Sweelinck; Johann Jacob Froberger (1616-1667) studied with Frescobaldi. Scheidt devoted his gifts to the church. His *Tabulatura nova* (3 volumes, 1624) and the *Tabulaturbuch* (1650) were important contributions to the new German church music; the latter comprised a hundred chorale settings, and formed a part of the literature of hymnody upon which a substantial amount of organ music was based. The chorale-prelude reached its zenith in the works of Dietrich Buxtehude (1637-1707), Johann Christoph Bach (1642-1703), Johann Pachelbel (1653-1706), Johann Gottfried Walther (1684-1748), and Johann Sebastian Bach (1685-1750).

The *chorale prelude* became a characteristically German organ form of the late Baroque. Treatment of the chorale was various. The tune might be put in the top voice in long notes, with a complex harmonization in shorter notes below; it might be given an ornamented, highly embellished variation, with a simple harmonization; it might provide a subject for a set of variations, or be set in canon or fugue. Techniques were based upon those used in similar paraphrases upon plainchant tunes by earlier composers, but the chorales lent themselves to a metric rhythm with ease, the phrases becoming subjects in learned or "worked" types of preludes. There was no limitation on the presentation of the chorale save that of the presence of the tune and the composer's imagination.

Like much of the Baroque creative process, the working out of chorales was related to the physical properties of the organ, both as a kind of tone quality and as an idiomatic instrument managed by a single person at a central control. Both were intensely concerned with contrasts: the ranks of pipes themselves embodied contrasts of quality, with wooden, metal, open, stopped, conical, cylindrical, and other classifications of pipes, placed architecturally for contrast of location and direction. The organist controlled the selection of sounds—in quality and location—both through activation of certain combinations and also by the use of two, three, or four manuals plus a pedal board. The physical separation of the various elements of the instrument was symbolized by the separation of controls and produced a further psychological separation of musical elements in the mind of the composer and organist; in a sense, the organ is truly a polyphonic instrument, dealing with layers of sound and layers of activity. Thus the organ chorale prelude remained polyphonic even when chorales were being sung in the new style.

Other forms still flourished as well—toccata, ricercar, organ canzona, fantasia—all the forms expanded. By the early years of the eighteenth century, they had polarized around two types: the free prelude, and the worked movement, most often a fugue. Two such movements arranged together could form a contrasting pair in the high Baroque sense. The first of the pair might be a prelude, toccata, fantasia, or even sinfonia— any movement based upon figured harmony, perhaps in lute style; the second was a fugue or a worked movement based upon a tone and subject.

Development of these forms lay in such works as those by Johann Jacob Froberger, and Georg Böhm (1661-1733), Dietrich Buxtehude, and J. S. Bach. The great works of the cantor of Leipzig brought the paired works to heights that have kept his organ compositions in the literature ever since. In his hands, the fugue was a structure in which the polyphonic Renaissance learned technique and the tonal-metric Baroque form—of subject and episode working out a tonal plan—coincided and reinforced each other to produce a uniquely satisfying total concept.

Example 10

Chorale and chorale prelude.

A. Chorale: *Ein feste Burg*, attributed to Martin Luther. From *Geist-reiches Gesang-Buch* (1674), by Christoph Bernhard.

Example 10—*Continued*

B. Treatment of a chorale phrase: the first phrase of *Ein feste Burg*, in works by several composers.

1. Schein, from the *Gesangbuch Augsburgischer Konfession* (1627) —note values halved. For voices and instruments.

Example 10—*Continued*

2. Scheidt, from the *Tablaturbuch* (1650)—note values halved. This is an organ setting.

3. Pachelbel, a fugal treatment. The entire movement deals with the first phrase only—this is the first third of the movement.

Example 10— *Continued*

4. From three harmonizations by J. S. Bach.

5. From J. G. Walther: a three-voiced chorale-prelude which puts imitative phrases in fast notes in the lower parts, using the upper part for slower, almost literal statements of the chorale, phrase by phrase.

Example 11

Prelude and Fugue for organ, by Johann Sebastian Bach—from the Eight Little Preludes and Fugues. This is a short work, intended for the student. Others were of much greater size.

Example 11– *Continued*

Example 11–*Continued*

Fuga.

Example 11– *Continued*

Example 11—*Continued*

THE FRENCH HARPSICHORD SCHOOL

The French court was a center of lute and guitar music. At the middle of the seventeenth century the *clavecin*, or harpsichord, rose to a position of prominence as a solo instrument. The aristocrat, Jacques Champion de Chambonnières (1602-1672), was a master harpsichordist to Louis XIII and then Louis XIV; *his pièces de clavecin* (harpsichord pieces) and skill in improvisation were virtually the foundation of the French harpsichord school, another great tradition of the late Baroque. Some two dozen composers contributed to that tradition, including Louis Couperin (1626-1661), Jean-Henry D'Anglebert (1628-1691, student and successor of Chambonnières), Elisabeth Jacquet de la Guerre (c. 1665-1729), and François Couperin (1668-1733), called "The Great," who was the harpsichord teacher to the Dauphin and Organist of the Royal Chapel. Couperin's four volumes of *Pièces de clavecin* (1713, 1717, 1722, 1730) and his text *L'art de toucher le clavecin* (The Art of Playing the Harpsichord, 1716) were highly regarded in his own day as well as in modern times.

The *pièce de clavecin* was most often a dance piece in the standard two-part form; the free-rhythm prelude, written in whole-notes, and the chaconne were used too. A native French form was the *rondeau*, a form of noble lineage stemming from the days of the Medieval *trouvères*. Its name indicated a "round form," in which repeated phrases combined with fresh ones. In the modern instrumental form a short, multiphrase section was the rondeau proper; it was played twice to begin the piece, and then it was followed by a section called a *couplet*, after which the rondeau was restated. Another couplet, another restatement of the rondeau, and so forth, ending with the rondeau, enabled the piece to achieve substantial size. By the end of the Baroque era, the rondeau was typically a lyrical movement with a rondeau and three or four couplets, and with some relation of subject between the first and third couplets, and often a variety of tonal levels as well.

French publications often presented a series of pieces in one tone, leaving the performer to select a number and order to make up a set or *suite* of pieces to suit himself. The tendency toward the middle of the eighteenth century, however, was to retain separate identities for pieces on the one hand and to create a short set of pieces to be played in a specified order on the other.

The separate pieces tended toward musical portraiture or depiction; pieces frequently had titles of persons—notable or notorious,—places, battles, occasions, emotions, or even animals. Most of the pieces by the great Couperin had such designations. The suites by Joseph Bodin de

Example 12

A. *Prélude* from *Pièces de clavecin* (1705), by Gaspard Le Roux; in the lute and harpsichord free style, it presents rhythmic suggestion by succession and by slurs and sustaining signs, but leaves details to the performer.

Prélude

The French harpsichord works most often used the first-line C clef (soprano) for the right hand and the third-line F clef (baritone)—the right hand begins *d-e-f♯*, and the left hand begins on G. The prélude is in g minor. The music is engraved—the most satisfactory technique for keyboard works, which demanded more than one note at once on a staff.

For a table of embellishments, see Plate VI-B, page 62.

Example 12—*Continued*

Prelude

Example 12—*Continued*

B. *Sarabande* from *Pièces de clavecin qui peuvent se Joüer sur le Viollon* (1707) by Elisabeth Jacquet de La Guerre.

In the usual soprano and baritone clefs, the Sarabande is also in the usual two-part form, with the first and second endings of the first section separated by a heavy vertical slash through half the staff, and the beginning of the second marked "Reprise" (repeat). In the French style, the last phrase was customarily repeated—the repetition was called the *petite reprise*. It was often indicated by a repeat mark, but in this case it is written out (the two phrases comprise the final eight measures), with differing harmonic goals. The embellishment in the right hand provides insight into figuration (*division* of the original); a *tirade* appears in the third measure from the end.

Although the Sarabande is in *d* minor, it begins in *D* major, showing that the *tones* of *d* minor and *D* major were already considered, within the French style, as alternative color in a single *key* of *D*.

Courtesy of the Bibliothèque Nationale, Paris.

Example 12– *Continued*

Example 12—*Continued*

C. *Gavotte* with the first two *Doubles* (variations), from *Nouvelles Suites de Pièces de Clavecin* (1728) by Jean-Philippe Rameau. The six doubles display sophistication and imagination, along with a modern and substantial keyboard technique. For Rameau's own instructions on playing the ornaments, see Plate VI-B, (page 62).

Boismortier (1691-1765) illustrates the tendency at the end of the Baroque. His suites Opus 59 (1736) contain four and five movements; all have titles in addition to tempo or dance designations (or both). The third is representative:

IIIe Suite.
  [1] *L'Impérieuse* (The Haughty One)
     Fièrement et piqué (Proudly and detached).
     (In *e*, 3 time; two-section form)
  [2] *La Puce* (The Flea)
     Pièce en rondeau.
     (In *e*, 8/6 Time; a rondeau of two couplets, with the rondeau notated each time as a variation of the original strain.)
  [3] *La Navette* (The Shuttle)
     Bourrée en rondeau.
     (In *e*, 2 time; a rondeau of two couplets, written normally with the rondeau proper notated but once.)
  [4] *La Flagorneuse* (The Flatterer)
     Pièce en rondeau
     (In *E*, 3/8 time; a rondeau of two couplets written normally.)
  [5] *La Belliqueuse* (The Belligerent, Warlike)
     Allemande - Vivement
     (In *E*, c time; two-section form)

The suite is typical in its allusions, including the "flea" and the "shuttle," which depict motions—an extremely disjunct subject with a constant crossing of hands. The large number of rondeau forms was not representative, however, though the presence of both two-section and rondeau forms was.

A late Baroque development in the French harpsichord school was the *pièce en concert*, combining the *pièce de clavecin* with other instrumental forms through the use of the violin, flute, or other instruments. Works of Elisabeth Jacquet de La Guerre were early in the new type; her *Pièces de clavecin* of 1707 specified the use of a violin, evidently doubling the melodic line of the harpsichord. The *Pièces de clavecin en sonates* (1738) of Jean-Joseph Cassanéa de Mondonville (1711-1772) combined the *pièce* with the solo violin sonata; and the *Pièces de clavecin en concert* (1741) by Jean Philippe Rameau (1683-1764) combined the *pièce* with the trio sonata.

In addition to the harpsichord music, a French organ school flourished as well. Such organists as Nicolas Lebègue (1631-1702), Nicolas de Grigny (1672-1703), and Louis-Nicolas Clérambault (1676-1749) brought French organ music to a particular height. The French brought

their love of color to bear upon the organ literature, specifying registra-
tion and composing especially in reference to it. They also cultivated
the variation of the *Noël* or folk tune with Christmas text. The organ
Noël remained a popular form in France through the eighteenth century.

In France, the harpsichord was at the center of French musical life;
the great virtuosos were playing large, two-manual instruments at the
concert hall or salon, and the small, one-manual instrument was the
new instrument of the home, played by gentle folk who bought the
pièces de clavecin published for their pleasure, and who also took pleasure in realizing figured basses in trio sonatas, often hiring professional
musicians to play the solo lines.

GERMAN KEYBOARD MUSIC

In Germany the keyboard tradition of home instruments centered in
the clavichord instead of the harpsichord. The clavichord was an intimate instrument whose soft, silky tone was extremely pliant and expressive. It was too delicate for concerts or large halls, or for combining
with other instruments, but it was ideal for the performer to play just
for himself.

The clavichord and harpsichord were both string instruments played
with keyboards, but their mechanism was different. The *harpsichord*
string was *plucked* by a *jack* mechanism, while the *clavichord* string
was *touched* with a *tangent;* the plectrum of the harpsichord jack en-
gaged the string in passing, while the clavichord tangent stayed on the
string as long as the key was held down. The concert harpsichord was
capable of considerable power, with two (or even three) manuals, and
great thrust, clarity, and resonance available through delineation of
attack. The clavichord was capable of great subtlety; the tangent, by
touching and remaining upon the string, determined its sounding length
but also deadened the tone. By varying the pressure on the key, the
player could influence intonation, and a quick alternating up-and-down
of the finger could create a vibrato, characteristic of the clavichord,
called the *Bebung.*

The rising middle classes in Germany provided the ideal home for
the clavichord, simply by having houses with small rooms (as distinct
from palaces with halls or salons), and the popularity of the clavichord
in the middle of the eighteenth century was largely that of the amateur,
the gentleman or *homme galant.*

Not as interested in color as the French, the Germans brought out
works for "clavier," that is, keyboard, without specification of instrument. The suites of Johann Jacob Froberger, published a generation
after his death, were keyboard works; much of the keyboard music of
Johann Caspar Ferdinand Fischer (c. 1675-1746) was unspecified, as

was the famed *Das wohltemperierte Clavier* (Well-Tempered Keyboard) of Johann Sebastian Bach. Fischer's *Ariadne Musica* had expanded the eight tones to twenty, and Bach's *Clavier* had expanded the concept still further, projecting each of the twelve notes of equal temperament as a possible tonic of both a major and a minor tone. The forty-eight preludes and fugues of Bach's *Clavier* were to remain in the amateur's bag of didactic necessaries, to become the pianist's "Old Testament" in the nineteenth century. (The Beethoven piano sonatas would become the "New Testament.")

J. S. Bach's son, Carl Philipp Emanuel (1714-1788), was an important composer of music for clavichord, preferring it to the harpsichord. He experimented also with the new-fangled *pianoforte* when he worked for Frederick the Great in Berlin (1740-1767); that instrument, a recent Italian invention, tried to combine the expressive power of the clavichord with the dynamic range of the harpsichord. Its mechanism differed from both: the *piano* string was *struck* by a *hammer*. The new instrument was initially built in the shape of a concert harpsichord and, perhaps because of its cost, got off to a slow start. It would be the development of a smaller, square piano modeled after the English spinet, that would signal the sudden popularity of the piano, to have its most intense career in the nineteenth century.

THE BRITISH SPINET

The British had enjoyed a great keyboard tradition at the end of the Renaissance in the small, portable box harpsichord called the *virginals.* Such composers as William Byrd (1543-1623) and Giles Farnaby (c. 1560-1640) created an art of dances, variations, and character pieces that comprised one of the glories of Elizabethan and Jamesian England.

At the end of the seventeenth century, after a lull in composing for the keyboard, the spinet became popular. This was wing shaped, with the player at the shorter of the two long sides and the strings running across, left and right, in front of the performer. The spinet was larger than the virginals but, with only one manual and with shorter strings, smaller than the large concert harpsichord.

English music at the end of the Baroque era was eclectic; the harpsichord music of George Frideric Handel (1685-1759) was basically Italian in style, as were the native works by Thomas Augustine Arne (1710-1778) and others, but they were also influenced by France and Germany. The career of Handel summed up this internationalism, as did the career of J. S. Bach's eleventh son (eighteenth child) Johann Christian (1735-1782). Born in Germany and trained there and in Italy, he made his career in London where he was an important composer in the transition to the coming Classical era. He gave the first known public piano recital in London in 1768.

THE ITALIAN SCHOOL

The music of the Italian harpischord school is associated universally with the name of Domenico Scarlatti (1685-1757), the son of the famed opera and cantata composer Alessandro. The young Domenico was famous at twenty, and at thirty-five was in the service of the Infanta of Portugal, later Queen of Spain. His reputation as a harpsichord virtuoso was international.

Scarlatti wrote many works; a few of his harpsichord pieces were published in his lifetime as *Essercizi per gravicembalo* (Studies for Harpsichord), in five volumes from 1738, but most of the surviving 550 remained in manuscript, to be published in modern times. (They are generally called "sonatas" today.) These were of many moods, but were unified in use of the two-section form. It is believed that Scarlatti played these movements in contrasting pairs—a likely practice in an era of contrasts.

Other Italians, such as Francesco Durante (1684-1755) brought harpsichord music to the edge of the Classical style. The combination of the Italian rhythmic drive with the harpsichord idiom produced a vigorous style and a clarification of the subject—and of the use of more than one subject—vital to the coming modernity.

SUGGESTIONS FOR FURTHER STUDY

Records

Bach (J. S.), Cantata #80, *"Ein feste Burg ist unser Gott."* Prohaska and the Akademiechor, Bach 508.
    The works of J. S. Bach are on Archive records.
French Harpsichord Masters. Lyrichord Discs, LL19.
French Organ Masterpieces of the 17th and 18th Centuries. Nonesuch H-1020.
Yale Collection of Musical Instruments, Vol. I. Works of Froberger, J. S. Bach, and Louis Couperin. Yale Collection of Musical Instruments, 15 Hillhouse Avenue, New Haven, Conn. YCMI 1.

Books and Music

Achtzig Choralvorspiele Deutscher Meister des 17, und 18. Jahrhunderts (Eighty Choral Preludes by German Masters of the 17th and 18th Centuries) edited by Hermann Keller (New York: C. F. Peters, 1937).
BACH, JOHANN SEBASTIAN. *371 Four Part Chorales* (2 Vols). New York: Edwin F. Kalmus, n.d.

————. *Inventionen und Sinfonien.* New York: C. F. Peters, n.d. A facsimile of the original, in Bach's hand.

————, *Orgelwerke* (Organ Works), edited by Friedrich Conrad Griepenkerl and Ferdinand Roitzsch. New York: C. F. Peters (#247), n.d.

BOISMORTIER, JOSEPH BODIN DE. *Quatre Suites de Pièces de Clavecin* (Four Suites of Harpsichord Pieces), *Op. 59, 1736,* edited by Erwin R. Jacobi. Munchen-Leipzig: Verlag von F. E. C. Leuckhart (Leuckartiana #26), 1959. Excellent edition.

BORROFF, EDITH. *An Introduction to Elisabeth-Claude Jacquet de La Guerre.* Brooklyn, N.Y.: Institute of Medieval Music, Ltd., 1966.

FRESCOBALDI, GIROLAMO. *Ausgewahlte Orgelwerke in Zwei Banden, Part I: Fiori Musicali* (1635). Selected Pieces for Organ in Two Volumes, edited by Herman Keller. New York: C. F. Peters (#4514), c. 1943.

LE ROUX, GASPARD. *Pieces for Harpsichord,* edited with a preface by Albert Fuller. New York: C. F. Peters (Alpeg Editions), c. 1959.

L'Orgue Parisien sous le Règne de Louis XIV (The Parisian Organ in the Reign of Louis XIV), edited by Norbert Dufourcq. Frankfurt, Germany: Wilheim Hansen (#4007), 1956.

TELEMANN, GEORGE PHILIPP. *Fantaisies Pour le Clavessin.* New York: Broude Brothers, n.d.

10

Opera at the
End
of the Baroque

THE ITALIANS—OPERATIC MASTERS OF EUROPE

 n the last third of the Baroque era, opera was at its height. Sonatas may have outnumbered all other musical types, and concertos may have pointed to the new modernity with special thrust, but opera was the one form that captivated the public as a total experience. The introduction of magnificent entertainments to a public both eager and able to pay was perhaps the most spectacular accomplishment of the Baroque era, symbolizing the social developments of a century and a half and the development of the middle class and its political power.

The center oi operatic creativity was Naples, where Alessandro Scarlatti (1660-1725), who wrote 115 operas, centered his later career. By the end of Scarlatti's life the Italian art of *bel canto* had defined a pedagogy, and the era of great teaching and great singing began. Italian teachers expanded over the European scene, as Italian singers had already done. A few non-Italians became opera singers (most of them took Italian names), but the great singers were still Italians. The greatest teacher was Nicola Antonio Porpora (1686-1767), who composed 53 operas and led an international career; like many Italians, he was employed by a German court, though he spent most of his life in Naples and Venice. He taught the best singers of the era, including the castrato Carlo Broschi, called Farinelli (1705-1782), considered by many the greatest of them all.

Johann Adolph Hasse (1699-1783), a German from Hamburg, represented another type of composer of Italian opera; he began as a singer (tenor) at eighteen in the German opera under Reinhard Keiser; but as though to presage the capitulation of German opera to Italian, Hasse composed his first opera in Italian (1721) and then went to Naples to study with Alessandro Scarlatti and Nicola Porpora. Though German born, he must be counted as an Italian opera composer, with works produced in Dresden, Paris, Brussels, Venice, and London,—in Italian, of course.

The opera was first and foremost a theatrical entertainment, in which the aural and visual elements—acts, costumes, machines—vied in elegance and effect. The aria had taken over the musical action, and the recitativo was secondary, no longer a means of dramatic reality but of musical contrast and theatrical connection between arias. The Italian

Plate XI

Performance of opera at Rome. Painting by Giovanni Paolo Panini, representing the production of *La Contese de' numi* by Leonardo Vinci (1690-1730), at the palace of Cardinal de Polignac, 1729.

opera was a series of set pieces connected by recitative, with the singer the glamorous star of the whole. At its height, it had been a spectacle of unified magnificence, in which the music balanced other elements in producing a splendid view of a mythological or legendary tale.

Only French opera was able to maintain a national character; it never yielded to the Italian, but continued to work out its own special interests: ballet, instrumentation, harmonic color, and, even when Italian recitativo was in a state of decline, the French recitative. The set piece in French opera was important, but the connections were fairly natural and the difference between recitative and aria was not as great as in Italian opera. The unique figure, Jean-Philippe Rameau (1683-1764), produced twenty-six operas after 1733 when he was fifty. These works were recognized for their originality in all the areas particularly French; a few of these, especially *Castor et Pollux* (1737), are among the great works of the century.

REACTIONS TO GRAND OPERA

The new middle classes responded enthusiastically to the spectacle of grand opera, but not to the increasingly trite plots. The early eighteenth century saw the birth of the novel, the literary genre of the common man. *Pamela, or Virtue Rewarded* (1740), a novel claimed to be the first, by Samuel Richardson (1689-1761), the story of a servant girl who maintains virtuous deportment in the face of her employer's advances, was a clarion recognition of the common man. Inevitably, reactions to grand opera became more strongly negative; in the second quarter of the eighteenth century, a popular musical theatre became established as a viable new type.

In Italy the new type was called *opera buffa,* a term denoting farce or buffoonery, and a misnomer for the type as a whole, though it did apply to some early examples. It was, in a sense, anti-opera, opposite to the grand productions in as many particulars as possible: short instead of long, simple instead of complex, about lowborn instead of highborn persons, a contemporary instead of a mythological or historical action. It was most likely an *intermezzo,* played between the acts of a grand opera, produced with a minimum of panoply, and sung with a directness required by its audience's delight in its timely and amusing libretto.

An early *opera buffa* served to capitalize thoughts about the new type in Italy and abroad; it became one of the most famous operas of the century and one of the earliest to remain in the operatic repertoire: *La Serva Padrona* (in English, *The Maid as Mistress*) by the Neopolitan composer, Giovanni Battista Pergolesi (1710-1736), who, in spite of the tragic brevity of his career, was one of the most widely performed composers of the mid-century. A two-act intermezzo produced in Naples in 1733, it immediately became popular there; it was done in Paris in Italian in 1748, and in French in 1752, and caused a furor which the French called *La Guerre des Buffons*, The War of the Buffoons.

The French had been seeing comic scenes at the *foires* or fairs, similar to State Fairs in their mixture of exhibits and theatrical variety shows. The *Théâtre de la Foire* (Theatre of the Fair) rivaled the legitimate theatres in popularity in the 1720's, presenting everything from magicians and rope-dancers to short comic skits. A skit, anything from three to ten minutes long, was called a *vaudeville*; the music for it was in the direct style of the popular song, and frequently found its way to the collection of popular songs published in a constant stream in Paris.

Charles-Simon Favart (1710-1792) was the figure who set the *Théâtre de la Foire* on a new path from haphazard scenes to genuine operatic production, proving to the French that opera need not have the heroic subjects, lavish productions, and high-flown singing that the "legitimate" opera demanded. Favart was a librettist and producer, and not a composer, but he brought good texts to good composers and made unified, artistically whole productions that were copied internationally—particularly in Germany—in the Classical era. He sought a permanent theatre building, and by 1750 was seeking to merge with the Italian .company in Paris.

In England, the reactions to grand opera were reactions not only to the lavish and postured productions, but were also to the domination of a foreign tongue on the English stage. The English maintained a lively tradition of folk and popular songs and ballads, and in 1728 the poet, John Gay, wrote some low-life dialogue to string together a group of popular songs and ballads chosen and arranged by a theatre musician named John Christopher Pepusch (1667-1752), calling his production *The Beggar's Opera*. It inaugurated a type called the *ballad opera* that combined dialogue and song. Perhaps the most widely performed ballad opera was *The Devil to-Pay* by Charles Coffey, produced in London in 1731 (in Charleston in 1736, New York in 1751), but later to appear also in French, Italian, and German versions which would cause that form to influence other national types in the Classical opera. In addition, a light opera developed, composed newly for a text in English by men like T. A. Arne; such a work was called an English or chamber opera.

The fact that grand opera was "Italian international" at the middle of the century was hardly surprising; international interactions in the popular theatre, however, were surprising because popular theatre depended upon topical and idiomatic language, and the text was important in a way that it was not in lavish productions. At the very end of the Baroque era, several international developments led opera to the threshhold of reform, a reform that would be a central accomplishment of musical Classicism.

At the end of the Baroque, Favart gained his long-sought merger with the Italian company who had brought *opera buffa* to Paris; the new company would be called the *Opéra-Comique*. In 1752 the encyclopedist, Jean-Jacques Rousseau (1712-1778), produced *Le Devin du Village* (The Village Seer), a popular song opera influenced by the English model: It would be done in London in 1766 as *The Cunning-Man*; and two years later, Favart's parody of it would be translated into German and set by the twelve-year-old Wolfgang Amadeus Mozart (1756-1791) as *Bastien und Bastienne*.

In Naples in 1754, the composer Niccolò Piccinni (1728-1800) produced the first of his 140-odd operas, while the German Christoph Willibald Gluck (1714-1787) was working in Vienna on French vaudevilles, including texts by Favart. The two men would pursue different directions: in 1760 in Rome Piccinni modified the grand opera style, producing Richardson's novel *Pamela* as *La buona figliuola* (The Good Girl); in Vienna Gluck sought new dramatic validity in his 1762 production of *Orfeo ed Euridice* (also in Italian). They would meet in rivalry in Paris a decade later, and their productions would be vital in new operatic styles whose fruition would await another century.

SUGGESTIONS FOR FURTHER STUDY

Records

    Haydn: *The Man in the Moon* (*Il Mondo della Luna*). Lyrichord, LL 120.
    Operas of Keiser, Handel, and Telemann, Angel, Ang 36273.
    Pergolesi: *La Serva Padrona*. Vox SOPX 50.380.

Other Forms at
the
End of the Baroque

SONATA AND CANTATA

The last decades of the Baroque era were those when interest in musical instruments (including the voice) and their deployment in contrasting sounds and groups gradually gave ground to interest in new musical textures, both structural and surface. These textures would define musical fabric and look anew at the idea of subject, particularly the use of one subject in relation to others. If any idea led into the new Classical style, it was the desire for expanded musical works, achieving size not through the addition of more and more sections, but through organic relationships of key center and of subject. The attainment of such forms was an accomplishment of Classicism; but the preparation of a vocabulary of techniques necessary to its attainment was central to the Baroque. Like all musical eras, it comprised a particular fruition of its own ideal on the one hand, and a bridge between two other ideals —Renaissance and Classical—on the other.

The sonata and cantata comprised the most completely Baroque forms in the sense that they incorporated a fruition of the Baroque ideal. In the larger sense, the solo sonata and the solo cantata, the trio sonata and the duet cantata (or solo cantata with a solo instrument) were sibling forms; only the medium was different—the fabric rather than the form. A late cantata such as Handel's *Nel Dolce dell' Oblio*, for soprano, recorder, and basso continuo, and his *Trio Sonata in F Major*, for violin, recorder, and basso continuo, are quite similar. They are most similar in structural texture, sharing the polar ideal in its expanded sound of double soprano plus melodic/harmonic bass. The two instruments in the treble were more common than one, and contrasting instrumentation was more common in France and Germany where amateurs provided a market for publications that were more likely to sell if they could serve violin, flute, and oboe equally well. The added voice or instrument served to allow fuller harmony and more versatile texture.

The Handel *Cantata* had four movements, two sets of recitative and aria; the *Trio Sonata* had five movements: Larghetto, Allegro, Adagio, Allegro, Allegro,—two slow-fast pairs plus a final contrasting fast movement.

Thus although the trio sonata could be interested in color, it was less interested in idiomatic writing for instruments, which would have been too difficult for amateurs and which might also limit sales.

The solo sonata enjoyed a new sort of success at the end of the Baroque: from Corelli's day it was a chief form of the virtuoso. The violin virtuoso was a rival to the singer, and by the middle of the eighteenth century, the flute was second in popularity. By 1740 over two dozen violinists—mostly Italian and French—were touring as virtuosos, writing their own works, and as public concerts increased in number, the number of soloists increased accordingly. Perhaps the greatest of these were the Italian Giuseppe Tartini (1692-1770), who wrote 150 solo sonatas; Jean-Marie Leclair (1697-1764), a Frenchman who was considered one of the best of a dozen or so French violinists but whose 47 sonatas made him the leader of composition for solo violin; and Francesco Geminiani (1687-1762), an Italian who had studied with Corelli and who took his art to Paris, Dublin, and London, where he taught. Solo sonatas for flute were common as well. Those of the Frenchman Michel Blavet (1700-1768) and the German Johann Joachim Quantz (1697-1773) set a high standard for the era.

The solo sonata, composed for a particular man and particular instrument, was not only idiomatic but individual—even eccentric. It complemented the more generalized trio sonata; it was difficult, specialized, with an inconspicuous basso continuo (which supported the solo rather than balancing it), and an interest in technical aspects of the instrument with which the virtuoso amazed his growing public.

The sonata for keyboard alone was the product of the clavichord composers of Italy and the German states; the latter transferred the expressive elements of the intimate instrument to the concert hall. In Italy, the keyboard sonata began with the harpsichord. The piano sonata had a great early exponent in Carl Philipp Emanuel Bach (1714-1788).

The cantata remained the chief solo vocal concert type in France, Italy, and England, and a church form in the German states. The oratorio, grand motet, and Passion were at their height, as another Baroque fruition—and of course, so was the opera. Popular song, pub-

Example 13

The solo sonata.

A. The *Vivace* of Sonata VII from *12 Sonatas or Solos for a Violin* (Opus 5) by Corelli, as published by J. Walsh in London about 1730. The edition was engraved.

A lively interaction between treble and bass is heightened by quick imitative subjects often appearing in sequence. The first part ends on the dominant with a Phrygian cadence (characterized by the bass descent from the lowered sixth to the dominant tone, most often as here with the 7-6 suspension). The repeat sign resembles its modern counterpart.

Example 13—*Continued*

B. The *Adagio* of the Sonata in D major from *Sonates Pour le Viollon et pour le Clavecin* by La Guerre (1707).

For linear treble instruments the French violin clef was used; it places g^1 on the bottom line (the first note of the violin part is a^1). Although La Guerre's sonata followed Corelli's and was influenced by his style, the publication preceded the Walsh edition by a quarter of a century; it thus demonstrates earlier practices in notation. The sharp and flat signs, for example, are used to raise or lower pitches (as in the bass $C\flat$ for $C\natural$ in Measure 2 and $B\sharp$ for $B\natural$ in Measure 9), and the natural sign was still rare. It was most often used to cancel a flat, as here in the violin part at Measure 6.

Differences between French and Italian practices in figuring the bass are few and in small points, but a typical French progression, at Measures 6 to 8 of the LaGuerre, shows the figure $x\overset{6}{4}$ at Measure 7 over a $B\flat$, to indicate a sixth and augmented fourth over the bass. The augmented fourth required no alteration, but is indicated by the notation, evidently for purposes of voice leading. A comparable chord, over a bass f, and figured $\frac{4}{2}$ without any indication of the character of the fourth, is found in the fifth score of the Corelli.

Courtesy of the Bibliothèque Nationale, Paris.

lished increasingly in both single sheets and collections, took to the concert hall as well, but more commonly to informal concerts. Popular outdoor concerts featured them—the most famous of these were the Promenade Concerts at London's Vauxhall Gardens, which ran from 1660 to 1859, and those at Marlebone, from 1650 to 1776.

CONCERTO GROSSO

At the end of the Baroque era it was the concerto which was being leavened most surely with the impulses of modernity and which would spill into the Classical era with a wide scope of types, eventually to outline the whole instrumental art of two centuries to come.

By Vivaldi's mature years the concerto was as diverse as his astounding fecundity could make it. His more than 450 works of that name defy any single definition of the type; they range in size from the *Concerto in g* (Ricordi #41) for flute, violin, and basso continuo of bassoon and harpsichord, to several works for solo violin with two *ripieno* groups. The concept of the concerto was extremely fluid, but as the first decades of the eighteenth century passed the concerto more and more certainly intimated things to come. The concerto grosso, in its original concept of concertino plus concerto grosso groups, was a quintessential Baroque type, but it did not thrive beyond the Baroque years.

The concerto grosso in the old sense was a lively member of Vivaldi's output. In his hands, two tendencies away from the old usage are clear: one was toward the larger concertino conceived as a variety of sounds to be tapped rather than as a unified group apposite to the concerto grosso; the other was the smaller concertino of two members, or, increasingly, of a solo, conceived as a more virtuoso element pitted against a larger (rather than balanced with a smaller) concerto grosso.

The larger concertino is represented in the *Concerto in F* (Ricordi #43) for 2 oboes, bassoon, 2 horns, solo violin, and a concerto grosso with parts for two violins, viola, cellos and basses, and continuo harpsichord. In this work, the concertino does not appear as a separate unit, but is variously deployed, or, in a ritornello or tutti section, joins with the concerto grosso in the total force. Deployments include: a solo trio of horns and bassoon; a separation of upper parts—solo violin, oboes, ripieno violins, and violas—without basses; a solo trio of oboes and bassoon; and, most important, use of the solo violin with continuo only (solo cello and harpsichord). The second, slow movement, as is common in the concertos, uses a reduced instrumentation, in this case an opening and closing tutti of all strings with continuo, and a central lyric section for solo violin and upper strings only. Such a work produces an effect of basic string choir with available woodwinds for variety and color, a concept virtually defining the Classical ideal of the orchestra.

Example 14

Concerto grosso texture. Opening five measures of the Vivaldi *Concerto in F major* (Ricordi #43).

The upper four staves of the example show the concertino of two solo oboes, a bassoon, two solo horns, and a violin. The lower four staves show the concerto grosso, which includes two violin parts, a viola part, and a bass part; the original part folder contained three copies of the bass, for cellos, double bass, and harpsichord (with figures, which do not show in the opening, since it is all on the tonic chord).

The opening two and a half measures are played *tutti*—by all. The solo trio of two horns and bassoon that follows (Measures 2 1/2-5) is the first deployment of the concertino, but, in a modern instrumental usage, within the ritornello section. In the later concerto grosso, the distinctions between the large and small groups were becoming less intense, both through such passages in the ritornelli and through the addition of part of the larger group to soloists in episodes. The blurring of the distinction is italicized here by the use of *f* and *p* in the tutti.

The open fifth at the end of the example, approached by the horns from a major third whose lower tone lies a fourth above that of the fifth, is idiomatic to brass music, where the instruments played open tones (partials); such progressions were called "horn fifths."

The *Water Music* (Concerto #25, 1717) of Handel and the *Brandenburg Concertos* (1721) of J. S. Bach represent the last stage of the concerto grosso and outline two types of modernity. The Handel achieves size through an accumulation of 20 movements; the separate movements are formally conservative, maintaining the old two-section dance forms,

Example 15

Double or duet concerto texture. Opening of the Vivaldi *Concerto in Bb major* (Ricordi #35), and the beginning of the first episode.

A. Opening tutti of the first ritornello section.

B. Beginning of the first episode. The two solo instruments play with the bass, now marked for solo cello and harpsichord only.

but are modern in the use of different wind instruments—flutes, oboes, trumpets, horns—in different movements. The Bach uses a variety of components (each of the six concertos has a different instrumentation), but each concerto is conceived traditionally in its instrumental deployment; its modernity lies in the virtuoso demands upon the soloists and in achieving size internally, by working over a movement's subject as though to explore its potential, and in bringing the ritornello form to its culmination.

SOLO CONCERTO

The solo concerto was the opposite of the concerto grosso in the matter of the concertino. It would survive because it was redefined as a solo vehicle, concerned with virtuosity rather than subject, texture, or total instrumentation. Vivaldi's output included over 40 violin concertos, several for bassoon, and some for other instruments. He himself was a violinist, so by far the greatest number of his concertos featured the violin.

Virtuoso performers wrote their own concertos as well as their own sonatas; the amazing Tartini left a hundred and forty violin concertos which were of great influence through the century. The ritornello form, a conservative structure, was extremely useful to the virtuoso: the ritornelli or tutti sections presented a subject and gave an overall tonal shape to the movement, while the episodes provided a fine mechanism for freewheeling busywork, idiomatic figurations, and other virtuoso effects. Even at the end of the eighteenth century, the solo concerto remained basically Baroque in form and in type in the hands of the flamboyant virtuosos, especially the violin virtuosos.

In France and the German states, the number of violin concertos was smaller than in Italy, but France also centered in the violin as a solo instrument; Leclair left a number of concertos. Both Bach and Handel wrote solo concertos, Bach's most famed were for harpsichord, Handel's for organ. Handel also wrote a concerto for harp. The German states were interested in the woodwinds and, at the end of the Baroque, the piano. The middle of the eighteenth century saw such men as Johann Wilhelm Hertel (1727-1789) writing concertos not only for their own instruments, but for others as well. But other virtuosos still specialized; the flutist Johann Quantz wrote over 200 concertos for one and two flutes.

At the end of the Baroque, the piano was coming into its own. C. P. E. Bach would compose 52 concertos for the new instrument. The piano was in the forefront of modernist developments, and from the beginning the solo piano concerto sought textures of the coming Classical style.

Example 16

Solo concerto texture. Openings of the three movements of the Vivaldi *Concerto in D major* (Ricordi #31). The second movement, undesignated in the original, is probably an Andante.

CHAMBER CONCERTO

Less easy to categorize in instrumentation was the small concerto, of a single group, trio, quartet, or quintet with basso continuo. These were by far the most various of the concerto types; many were trio sonatas, but generally with a difference. The *Concerto in g* (Ricordi #41) of Vivaldi is for flute, violin, and continuo specifying bassoon and harpsichord; the bassoon part is separate from the continuo harpsichord bass, often dividing and frequently remaining in the group while the harpsichord drops out. The parts with harpsichord serve as *ritornelli*, and the slow movement omits the harpsichord altogether. The *Concerto in D* (Ricordi #39) is for flute, violin, and bassoon or cello, but has no harpsichord—a trio rather than a trio sonata.

Others were quartets with or without continuo; the *Concert in D* (Ricordi #42), uses flute, oboe, violin, and bassoon with harpsichord, and features the flute; the second movement is for flute and bassoon without continuo. An identical instrumental component, *Concerto in B♭* (Ricordi #40), features violin and flute and uses a full instrumentation in the slow movement.

The *Concerts Royaux* (Royal Concertos, 1715) of Couperin were in the same tradition, and some of the sonatas were as well; the Sonata called *La Steinkerque* (from the Battle of Steinkirch, 1725), was for flute, oboe, bassoon, and *clavecin* continuo.

The combinations of instruments seem endlessly inventive; they led to the trio, quartet, and quintet types that would form the basis of chamber music in the Classical art to come.

The French had been writing "concerted" works centering in the harpsichord—the *pièces de clavecin en concert*. Mondonville's *pièces* were orchestrated and called *concertos* in performance. A later set of *pièces en concert* combined solo voice and violin, and that too, in a review of 1747, was called a "kind of concerto."

It was a Silesian working in Paris who carried the *pièce de concert* to the edge of the Classical style: Johann Schobert (c. 1735-1767) left twenty books of such works. Those with two added instruments were called "sonatas," those with more, "concertos" (some for violin, two horns, and harpsichord). The child Mozart played for Schobert in Paris during the Mozart family visit of 1762-1763, and in his early piano concertos he used Schobert's subjects.

In Germany, the small concerto had a prodigious practitioner in Georg Philipp Telemann (1681-1767), who called solo concertos "concertos" and the chamber concertos "overtures," of which (along with larger instrumentations) he wrote over 600. Some of these were *Tafelmusik*, table or banquet music, entertainments for the dinner table.

Example 17

Chamber concerto texture.

A. Opening of the Vivaldi *Concerto in g minor* (Ricordi #41) for flute, violin, bassoon, and harpsichord. (The last two form the basso continuo, but are specified.)

The *concertato* principle is carried out through contrasts of instruments, as in the opening double phrase: the first two measures use flute and basso continuo, and the next two use violin and basso continuo.

B. Opening of Vivaldi's *Concerto in B♭ major* (Ricordi #40) for flute, oboe, violin, bassoon, and harpsichord. (The latter two comprise the basso continuo, which has separate parts, the solo bassoon providing a more ornate version of the same general line.) The next phrase is for violin and basso continuo.

The smaller contingents used in entertainments led to an important type, particularly in Austria—the *divertimento*, also called *serenade*, *cassation*, or *notturno*. This was a chamber form of a string of movements related to concerto and dance traditions (particularly the minuet), generally one—but sometimes two—players to a part. Many experiments in the divertimento helped to prepare composers for the new style. The young Franz Joseph Haydn (1732-1809), a choirboy in Vienna in the 1740's, composed many such works in the 1750's, experimenting with recitative techniques for the violin, the use of brass instruments, and other innovations.

Probably the most popular master of the divertimento was Leopold Mozart (1719-1787), who was a famed violinist and orchestra conductor in Salzburg. His divertimenti, many on programs which he published in advertisements, were imaginative and well wrought, and much appreciated in his day.

CONCERTO RIPIENO

The chamber concerto was an expansion of the role of the concertino; its counterpart was the *concerto ripieno*, an expansion of the role of the larger group, the concerto grosso itself.

In Vivaldi's and Telemann's concertos, the basic group—often the entire group—was a string trio or quartet with continuo: two violin parts and a cello part, with or without a viola part, and often with the cellos doubled by the string bass. The separation of cello and bass was extremely rare: in Vivaldi's *Concerto in d* (Ricordi #36) for string

Example 18

Concerto ripieno texture.

A. Opening of the Vivaldi *Concerto in B♭ major* (Ricordi #32) for strings and harpsichord.

This is a typical concerto allegro figure, in interchange between the violin parts. The group is simply a concerto grosso without a concertino.

Example 18— *Continued*

B. Openings of the first and second movements of the Vivaldi *Concerto in d minor* (Ricordi #36) for strings and harpsichord, subtitled "Madrigalesco."

The opening movement is in the style of an Italian chromatic madrigal of the end of the Renaissance, and, in keeping with that style, begins with a slow movement in the familiar rhythmic technique, forming one of the rare slow openings in Vivaldi's concertos.

The second movement is a fugue in the French style, with subject and countersubject appearing together in the beginning.

---

quartet ripieno and continuo, the basses drop out for a single three-measure phrase in a fugal counterpoint in the first movement and for the opening eighth-note in the finale; in the *Concerto in c* (Ricordi #32), for the same component, there is no separation at all. As a general rule, the bass was considered still as a balance to upper parts, with double basses added for a more substantial upper element and often omitted in the slow movement when the number of instruments was reduced.

Of Vivaldi's fifty-odd *concerti ripieni,* a few added wind instruments not as a competing concertino but as part of the total ensemble. Such a group was no longer a concerto grosso but an orchestra in the modern sense. The definition of the orchestra was the culminating achievement of the Baroque era, and upon the establishment of this component and an initial exploration of its special form—the symphony—the Baroque style rose to a crest whose breaking would be the coming Classicism.

The orchestra and the symphony resulted from the joining of disparate elements. The opera was a primary source; its instrumental overture, dances, and interludes had provided a vivid showcase for instrumental experiments. Lully and his immediate successors had still thought in consorts, with the strings reinforced but winds generally single. Rameau was one of the consummate colorists of Western music, many later basic instrumental effects were innovated by Rameau in his remarkable opera orchestrations.

The opera contributed the overture form as well, generally a three-movement format of contrasting sections: slow-fast-slow in France and fast-slow-fast in Italy. The overture was often labeled *symphonie* or, in Italian, *sinfonia,* a general term for a mixed instrumental group or any of the interludes it provided in an opera, oratorio, motet, or cantata.

The divertimento provided a ready place to experiment in the combining of winds and strings in the new style, and it provided the idea of mixing types of movements—an Italian allegro, a French *minuet,* a fugue, a *rondeau,* perhaps another *minuet,* and a final quick dance, possibly a *jig* or *gigue.*

The French had been listening to such pieces since the turn of the century. Louis XIV had enjoyed Lalande's *Symphonies pour le souper du Roy* (Symphonies for the King's Supper), banquet suites in the tradition of the divertimento. But Mouret's *Concerts de chambre* (c. 1720) and his *Suites de symphonies* (1729) definitely looked forward to the symphony. And Boismortier's *Sonates pour les violons* (Opus 34, c. 1733) claimed on their title page to be for various instruments and to be "elegantly worked." By mid-century the symphony was defined, and when the young Belgian François-Joseph Gossec (1734-1829) arrived in Paris in 1751, he could begin the series of works that inaugurated the Classical symphony in France.

Like other modern forms, the symphony was worked out in musical enclaves where wealthy patrons supported exceptional groups of experimentors. Most of these were court establishments, but Gossec's patron was a tax-collector, Alexandre-Jean-Joseph Le Riche de La Pouplinière (1693-1762), a wealthy amateur who hired Rameau and then Gossec to direct his private orchestra. Another was the court of Frederick the Great at Berlin, where Carl Philipp Emanuel Bach carried on his experiments with music for the piano, and the flutist Johann Joachim Quantz served as tutor and composer to the amateur-flutist King. A third was the German court at Mannheim, where the Duke, Carl Theodore, maintained a musical group exceptional in both size and originality. The Czechoslovakian-born violinist, Johann Stamitz (1717-1757), at Mannheim from 1745, introduced orchestral techniques that made Mannheim the talk of musical Europe. Stamitz composed about 75 works called symphonies, for orchestral trio and quartet, often with added winds. A handful of Mannheim composers would contribute important works to the growing form.

In Great Britain, sponsorship was lacking for such productions at the middle of the century (though a generation later, the London concerts would make up for it); the organist, William Boyce (1710-1779), found plentiful support for his theatre pieces, his songs, and his church music, but his remarkable volume of eight *Symphonies* (1750) seem to have been ignored by a public interested in opera, oratorio, songs, and anthems. It was the symphonic output of the "London Bach," Johann Christian, that would establish the symphony in the British Isles and, by dint of emigrating musicians, in the New World.

In Austria all of the necessary ingredients were at hand; both Italian and French opera (grand and popular), the concerto, *Tafelmusik,* the new pianoforte sonatas, and the native divertimento came together. The geniality, ingenuity, instrumental boldness, and textural modernity of these elements were ready for the masters who would bring them together.

SUGGESTIONS FOR FURTHER STUDY

Records

J. S. Bach: *Brandenburg Concertos, complete.* Westminster XWN 2219.

J. S. Bach: *Dramma per Musica, the Contest between Phoebus and Pan* (Cantata No. 201). Bach Guild, Vanguard Recordings BG-514.

Campra, Mouret, Gautier: Motets for soloist and orchestra. Musical Heritage Society MHS 515.

Eighteenth Century Chamber Music for Wind Ensemble. Michael Haydn: Divertimento in D Major. Carl Stamitz: Quartet in E-flat Major Op. 8, No. 2. Karl Ditters von Dittersdorf: Partia in D Major, Divertimento in B Major. Music Guild M-28.

François Francœur: *4 Sonates pour Violon and Basse Continue. Société* Française du Son Artistique 174.155.

Handel: *Cantata: Nel Dolce Dell' Oblio; Sonatas in d Minor and C Major; Trio Sonata in F Major.* Counterpoint Esoteric Records, 1313 N. Vine St., Hollywood, Calif. 5515. Excellent.

Mondonville: *3 Sonates Pour Orchestre, extraites de Sei Sonate a Quattro.* Societe Française du Son Artistique, SXL 20.178.

Leopold Mozart, Divertimento and Serenade, Archive ARC 3093.

Stoelzel: *Concerto for 6 trumpets, 4 kettledrums, 2 harpsichords, and double string orchestra.* Mercury MG50385.

Symphonies of William Boyce, Decca DX105.

Vivaldi: *Concerto in F major, for 2 oboes, bassoon, 2 horns, violins, and concerto grosso* (Ricordi #43) Washington Records WLP-406.

Vivaldi: *The Four Seasons.* Mercury SRW 18041. Telemann: *Doppelkonzert fur Blockflöte, Querflote, Streicher, und Basso Continuo.* A superlative performance; the Double Concerto, for Flute, Recorder, and Concerto Grosso, incorporates the instrumental contrasts and vigorous beat of the Baroque at its best. Das Alte Werk 9413 B.

Music

BACH, JOHANN SEBASTIAN. *Brandenburgische Konzerte.* Leipzig: Edition Peters, 1947. A facsimile of the original, in Bach's hand.

LA GUERRE, ELISABETH JACQUET DE. *Sonata in D Major for Violin and Keyboard* (1707), edited by Edith Borroff. Pittsburgh: University of Pittsburgh Press, 1961.

~ఴ⋒ఴ~ 12 ~ఴ⋒ఴ~

At the Edge
of a
New Style

A NEW GENERATION IS READY

he techniques were ready, the goals were set. Two more requirements were also being fulfilled: the definition of a philosophy of music that would serve the new art, and the consummation of a pedagogy that could inform it.

The philosophy centered in a view of music as a working out of musical elements, notably subject within a meter and harmonic functions within a key. In a new Classical style, the idea of polarity of harmonic bass and melodic treble would be replaced by a concept of musical space stratified in a general way into three layers, roughly high, middle, and low, any of which might carry the functions of melody or harmony. The excitement lay in the musical ideas, the interplay of key and subject, conceived separately from their instrumentation even when wedded to it. It was thus to be more abstract than Baroque structures, which more often resulted from interplay of the performing forces themselves. The basso continuo—not just its notated form of figured bass—was discontinued as functions requiring notation entered the middle range and the harmonic aspects were no longer always in the bass.

The pedagogy was essentially Baroque, a polarity of the old and new. A two-fold discipline of the learned style of the Renaissance and of figured bass, both abstracted from stylistic embodiment, provided the basis of musical study for the next two centuries. The great text of the learned style was the *Gradus ad Parnassum* (Steps to Parnassus—a common text-book title) by the Viennese composer, Johann Joseph Fux

131

Plate XII

Gentleman playing the violin. Engraving from the *Versuch einer gründlichen Violinschule* (Treatise on the Fundamental Principles of Violin Playing) by Leopold Mozart. This illustration of the correct manner of holding the violin appeared in the first edition, 1756, but this facsimile is taken from the edition of 1770.

Courtesy of the Stellfeld Purchase, The University of Michigan Library, Ann Arbor. Photo by R. E. Kalmbach.

(1660-1741). The great work of the harmonic style was Rameau's *Traité d'harmonie* (Treatise on Harmony, 1722). The Fux was a textbook and has been used directly and in translations and adaptations since that time; such study was called *counterpoint*. The Rameau was a speculative work whose influence has been indirect. Its theory of *invertibility* enabled pedagogues to use the notation of figured bass in a new definition, fruitful in harmonic exercises and in harmonic analysis. The Rameau was not used directly, but, from the 1750's, has been the basis of virtually all texts in the study of *harmony*. These two studies, harmony and counterpoint, were considered at the middle of the eighteenth century, to cover the learned and the practical, and to deal with voices and instruments, but as the concept of music became more abstract, they were considered to represent the vertical and horizontal dimensions of musical space.

By 1750, the young Franz Joseph Haydn, fleeing from the danger of castration (because of his reputation as a choir boy), could get a copy of Fux, a book on thoroughbass, and the modern piano sonatas of C. P. E. Bach, and teach himself the art of music. In that same decade, three great treatises would complete the pedagogic basis of the new style: they were the violin treatise by Leopold Mozart, the keyboard treatise by C. P. E. Bach, and the flute treatise by Johann Joachim Quantz. All of them centered on a particular instrument, but dealt with the complete musical art.

THE SPIRIT OF THE BAROQUE

The spirit of an era cannot be summarized, but must be captured in numberless experiences, above all, of listening to—of meeting—many works written to embody it. The Baroque was a time of invigoration, of delight in diversity, and of wide-ranging experiment. Its key word would be *life*—of pulse and color, of freedom from inhibition, not only life, but *love of life*. An unquenchable reaching for experience, admiration for spontaneity, and joy in knowledge for its own sake were the Baroque at its best.

Musical style at the height of the Baroque embodied these traits: above all it throbbed with life, it reveled in tempo and beat, it took delight in instrumental diversity and color, and it cherished improvised variation and spontaneity of interpretation. To the extent that these qualities are unavailing in notation, the Baroque era is obscure, but to that same extent it is accessible to re-creation through spirited performance with particular immediacy.

The musicians of the seventeenth century invented recitative, cantata, opera, oratorio, solo and trio sonata, and concerto grosso. They defined meter and tone, and redefined the Renaissance structures—notably the two-section dance form and polyphonic types—in accommodation with the new theory. They devised the aria da capo, the ritornello and rondeau, and the overture forms. And they subjected the various musical instruments, including the human voice, to scientific probings, developing the greatest skill of instrument making known in the Western world.

Their legacy to their successors was huge: they began with the Renaissance band, invented the concerto grosso, and handed the orchestra to their heirs; they began with motets and madrigals, devised monody as combining vocal and instrumental forces, expanded this concept to the oratorio, and gave it to the world complete; they inherited the modes, worked in tones, and ended by defining keys; they took proportions and defined meters; and they took disparate instruments with a generalized instrumental style and developed particular idiomatic, then virtuoso techniques. They instituted a musical vocabulary and theory that would serve both Classic and Romantic eras, and developed a pedagogy to fulfill it. Above all they produced a host of works, small as a solo sonata and large as an oratorio, that are still as full of zest as when they were first heard, possessing that first excitement of the new vocabulary and its intimations that made Baroque musicians aware that they were living in exhilarating times.

SUGGESTIONS FOR FURTHER STUDY

Books

BACH, CARL PHILIPP EMANUEL. *Essay on the True Art of Playing Keyboard Instruments,* translated and edited by William J. Mitchell. New York: W. W. Norton & Company, Inc., 1949.

MOZART, LEOPOLD. *A Treatise on the Fundamental Principles of Violin Playing,* translated by Editha Knocker. New York: Oxford University Press, 1951.

QUANTZ, JOHANN JOACHIM. *On Playing The Flute, translated and with an introduction and notes by Edward R. Reilly.* London: Faber & Faber, Ltd., 1966. The notes are extremely valuable.

General Book List

BUKOFZER, MANFRED. *Music in the Baroque Era.* New York: W. W. Norton & Company, Inc., 1947.

DAVISON, ARCHIBALD T. and WILLI APEL. *Historical Anthology of Music,* Volume II. Cambridge: Harvard University Press, 1950. Over half of this volume is Baroque music.

GEIRINGER, KARL. *The Bach Family.* New York: Oxford University Press, 1954.

GROUT, DONALD JAY. *A Short History of Opera.* (2 Vols.) New York: Columbia University Press, 1947.

JANSON, H. W. *History of Art.* Englewood Cliffs, N. J.: Prentice-Hall, Inc., 1962.

MARCUSE, SIBYL. *Musical Instruments: A Comprehensive Dictionary.* New York: Doubleday & Company, Inc., 1964. Excellent.

NAGLER, A. M. *A Source Book in Theatrical History.* New York: Dover Publications, Inc., 1952. Both late Renaissance and Baroque chapters are illuminating on early opera.

PALISCA, CLAUDE. *Baroque Music.* Englewood Cliffs, N. J.: Prentice-Hall, Inc., 1965.

PINCHERLE, MARC. *An Illustrated History of Music,* translated by Rollo Myers. New York: Reynal & Company, 1959.

ROWEN, RUTH HALLE. *Early Chamber Music.* New York: Columbia University Press, 1949.

SACHS, CURT. *The Commonwealth of Art.* New York: W. W. Norton & Company, Inc., 1946.

SORELL, WALTER. *The Dance Through the Ages.* New York: Grosset & Dunlap, Inc., 1967. Beautifully illustrated, with substantial material on the seventeenth and eighteenth centuries.

STRUNK, OLIVER. *Source Readings in Music History.* New York: W. W. Norton & Company, Inc., 1950. The Baroque section is available separately in paperback.

Index

A

acoustics, 53
adagio
 mood, 31
 musical example, 44
 sonata da camera, 49
 sonata da chiesa, 43
Adams, John
 on the singing in a village church, 83
"Affetti Musicali" (1617), 42
Agnus Dei, 2
air
 comparison of national styles, 25
 equal importance with recitative, 30
 Krieger, 28
air de cour, 22
air mesurée, 24
allegro
 in the divertimento, 128
 mood, 31
 musical example, 44, 45
 sonata da chiesa, 43
alto, voice
 French choir, 40
anthem
 Renaissance music, 2
 use in England, 38
antiphon, 2
appoggiatura, 59, 62, 63, 67
apprentice, 38
aria, 14
 cantata, 38
 equal importance with revitative, 30
 French opera, 112
 Italian opera, 111
 Scarlatti, 37
 Schütz, 41
 SEE ALSO air
"Arianna" (1608), 9

Arne, Thomas Augustine (1710-1778), 107
 chamber opera, 113
"L'art de toucher le clavecin" (1716) (Couperin), 99
"L'Art du facteur d'orgues" (illustration), 87
"Augsburgischer Konfession" (1627) (Schein), 28
ayre
 in the popular English style; Renaissance music, 2

B

"B minor mass," 39
Bach, Carl Philipp Emanuel (1714-1788), 107, 116
 at the court of Frederick the Great, 128
 basis of the new style, 133
 composed concertos for the piano, 122
Bach, Johann Christian (1735-1782), 107, 108, 129
Bach, Johann Christoph (1642-1703), 88
Bach, Johann Sebastian (1685-1750), 38, 88, 89, 93, 94
 "Brandenburg concertos," 120
 "Das wohltempeirerte Clavier"; son of (Emanuel); eighteenth child (Christian), 107
 solo concertos for the harpsichord, 122
bagpipe
 most popular folk instrument, 76
ballad opera, 113
ballet (ballet de cour)
 France, 22
 spectacle; subjects of; popularity of, 24

137